When the Brook Runs Dry

My Journey from Africa to America...and
Back a Few Times

A Memoir

Alice Chidzero

When The Brook Runs Dry

Published by:
NyreePress Literary Group
Fort Worth, TX 76161
1-800-972-3864
www.nyreepress.com

ISBN print: 978-1-945304-93-4

Library of Congress Control Number: pending
Categories: Non-Fiction / Memoir / Self-Help / Christian
Printed in the United States of America

CPSIA information can be obtained
at www.ICGtesting.com
Printed in the USA
BVHW02s1342050218
507232BV00005B/7/P

Felix carrying Shekinah

Me carrying my late daughter Vimbai & my late husband and Simba

My father and mother

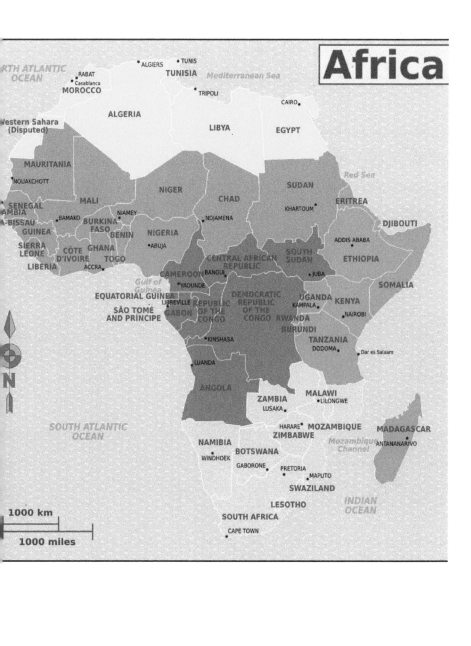

Now Elijah the Tishbite, of Tishbe in Gilead, said to Ahab, "As the Lord, the God of Israel, lives, before whom I stand, there shall be neither dew nor rain these years, except by my word." And the word of the Lord came to him: "Depart from here and turn eastward and hide yourself by the brook Cherith, which is east of the Jordan. You shall drink from the brook, and I have commanded the ravens to feed you there." So he went and did according to the word of the Lord. He went and lived by the brook Cherith that is east of the Jordan. And the ravens brought him bread and meat in the morning, and bread and meat in the evening, and he drank from the brook. And after a while the brook dried up, because there was no rain in the land. (1 Kings 17:1-7)

Dedication

To Lesley C. Hamer
For your friendship, I am eternally grateful. You have stood by
me like a sister, through good times and tough times! Thank
you!

and

To my son Simbarashe and my daughter Shekinah
Rumbidzaishe, you brighten my life and help me to keep going.
I love you both!

and

To my Lord and Savior Jesus Christ who has sustained me and
given me strength to complete this book! All glory and honor to
you.

Table of Contents

Forward

Often it is not until we are faced with difficult life circumstances that provide us nowhere to run or hide, that we call upon a being higher than ourselves. It is not until we see no way out that we call upon the hand of God, Buddha, Mary mother-of-Jesus or whoever it is we believe will provide what we need at the time to survive. It is human nature. We depend mostly on ourselves. We feel equipped, for whatever reason, to handle what life throws at us with very little help from others. It too often takes immense distress or turmoil in our lives to cause us to bow to an authority bigger than ourselves that can comfort and restore us. It sometimes takes a paralyzing event before we realize the meaning of life itself and the role we play in it.

Turbulence and instability, I think are God's tools to help us get to the end of ourselves quickly so we will search for truth and comfort in Him. The Bible even tells us to consider it pure joy, when we face trials of MANY kinds, because we will know

that it is the testing of our faith that will produce perseverance in us. That perseverance brings us to maturity, helping us to lack nothing. In the latter of James chapter one, the Bible tells us to call upon God, and in so doing, believe and not doubt, because if we doubt, we become like a wave in the sea, blown and tossed by the wind. With this kind of doubt, we are unable to clearly believe enough to receive what we need from Him.

Uncertain circumstances will come to each of us at one time or another. This is life. What we do when those times come, I believe, makes a difference of life or death for us. To have fullness of life, we must surrender and give ourselves back to the one who gave us life to begin with. Why, then, do some of us respond so quickly to this notion and others of us…never! I believe that because we are made in the image of Christ, there must be a part of Him in our DNA that calls out to Him for peace, hope, love and fellowship. Our soul in its most basic form can only be set to rest by the creator of it, Jesus Christ. Psalm 100 says that it is He who has made us, and we are His.

David, in Psalm 139, states clearly how well acquainted God is with us. "You have searched me, Lord and you know me. You know when I sit and when I rise; you perceive my thoughts from afar. You discern my going out and my lying down; you are familiar with all my ways. Before a word is on my tongue you, Lord, know it completely. You hem me in behind and before, and you lay your hand upon me. Where can I go from your Spirit? Where can I flee from your presence? If I go up to the heavens, you are there. If I make my bed in the depths, you are there. If I rise on the wings of the dawn, if I settle on the far side of the sea, even there your hand will guide me, and your right hand will hold me fast."

So the choice remains ours when we are faced with a fight in life: will we fight, will we run, or will we scream for help? In whom will we place our hope?

My story led me to Christ at every turn, it just took me awhile to see Him standing right in front of me with arms opened

wide. My story, is really simple and not at all complicated or even that unusual. I hated to fight. I hated confrontation. I hated conflict. Simple disagreements even bothered me. Fighting as a child in my family was a way of life. Okay, pretty similar story to many. You had to fight for what you needed to survive. If you needed something…anything, you had to fight for it! You had to fight to get food at the dinner table, fight to get into the bathroom and even fight to be heard over the other eight people who occupied my home. It was loud, chaotic and always unpredictable. Not only was fighting inside my home commonplace, but that was also true for my life outside of my home. In 5th grade I was welcomed into my neighborhood by a group of girls who beat the daylights out of me. Physically fighting the kids in my neighborhood was just how it was. If you had what it took to stand up and fight back, they would eventually leave you alone. The worst part was, my parents witnessed it but did not intervene because they knew it was something we had to conquer in order to survive in that particular community. After all, I lived on Chapel Street, not Park Avenue. I hated fighting but that was part of my upbringing, part of my community – it was life. I had to rely on myself.

By the time I was 13, I met Christ and discovered that there was someone who would do my fighting for me. He convinced me that if I trusted him with my life, all fighting as I knew it could cease. He convinced me that I would never have to go it alone, and I could be stronger with His help. I believed Him, gave my life to Him and everything has changed.

Fast forward thirty-two years. I meet a woman who fought her battles in a way that would always end in victory. This woman faced more obstacles than most people could ever begin to comprehend. A woman with whom my soul found instant love. The death of a child. The death of a husband. Living alone as a single mother in a foreign country. She had no place to run and certainly no place to hide. Like me, she hated fighting. She never wanted to claw and scratch and yell and scream to survive. Like me, she has had to fight for the greater portion of her life. Unlike

me, she understood why she had to fight and knew exactly what weapons were required for this kind of warfare.

Alice Chidzero is a mighty woman of faith. She has endured much stress and a life filled with turmoil. She however, has never lost sight that the battle was and is never against flesh and blood, but the battle is a spiritual battle. She is a woman who trusts God and believes in His faithfulness. Since I have known her, she has always been a person who had leaned on the promises of God and not her feelings or emotions.

Her story is unique, but so is her faith. I invite you to read about her life's journey.

Susan Anderson Oweis

Prologue

That night as I wrestled with sleep, I kept thinking about the baby we had buried that day. It was raining outside our apartment in Glen Norah and my baby was alone in the graveyard, covered with the thick blanket of dirt we had thrown onto her small white coffin. Next to me, my five-year old son, Simba slumbered, unaware of the seismic shift in our lives, on a small mat near the foot of the bed shared by my husband, Felix, and me. In the quiet of the apartment, I could hear their breathing, one heavy and raspy, and the other, light as a small finger. Unlike myself, Felix had fallen asleep immediately, exhausted from preparing for the funeral with the other men in the city. While there are funeral homes and directors in Zimbabwe, most of the responsibility lies with the family of the dead to take care of the details of the burial. It falls on the husband, family friends and uncles and grandfathers who, on the first night, build a fire and huddle together in the flickering light to work out the details of the burial.

The women's job was to take care of me, the mother, in shock and inconsolable. Every day since my daughter's death, the women in my life, connected to me by blood, by marriage or by divine appointment, had gathered with me, in the living room of my mother-in-law's house. The room had been emptied of all its furniture, and there, we cried, and wailed and danced, and when the wave of crying began to drown us all, to sing. It would go on all night long, the men around the fire, the women in the house, all of us preparing for the thing we did not want to do.

Later that night as the droplets tapped the window, unable to sleep, I found myself replaying scenarios from the day. Every muscle in my body, every thought in my head, told me to bring my daughter in where it was safe and dry, to protect her. But I could not bring her in, just as I could not keep her from dying. As the soft wail of the occasional car passed outside the window and mingled with the soft rhythm of the rain, I realized this is what life had given me. As much as I wanted things to be different, as much as I wanted my daughter to be here in the warm bed, her small body wedged between her father and me, her small fingers curled in sleep, it was not to be. My job, like that of all who have lost a child, was to find a path through the forest of pain and move forward. I knew that God would help me. At the moment, however, I just didn't know how.

Chapter 1
A Little Girl in Rhodesia

G rowing up in rural Rhodesia in the 1960s, I was insulated from the unrest that was brewing in the cities. As the youngest of nine children, I knew we were under British rule, but that did not concern me because we always had shoes to wear and a roof over our heads. In our case, the roof was made of zinc. There was no ceiling to shield the living space and, to this day, the loud patter of rain on a metal surface takes me back to those early years in Gutu.

Both of my parents were Shona, the largest ethnic group in Zimbabwe. My father served as pastor of a Dutch Reformed Church. While it is typical for Shona children to be named for a desirable character trait (e.g., "Knowledge", "Compassion", and even "Marvelous"), my parents' faith is reflected in the names they gave to my eight siblings. Their firstborn, Jacob, is 20 years older than me. He was followed by Obadiah, Alpha (the first girl), Christine (so named because she was born on Christmas day), Levi (also my father's name), Precious, and Jephta (better known

by his Shona name Njodzi which means danger). I was told that my mother had suffered a serious stroke after Jephta's birth. Four years later, however, she gave birth to my brother Benjamin. She produced her ninth and last child in 1963. I was named by my sister Alpha and that is how I ended up with a name that did not seem to fit with the rest of the family. Most of my family members have two names, the "English" one and the Shona name. My Shona name, Rumbidzaishe, means "Praise the Lord". All of my parents' children were healthy; none was disabled in any way, and my name demonstrated my parents' gratitude for this great blessing. By the time I was three years old, my parents' first grandchild was born, so I did not enjoy the spotlight accorded to the youngest child for long.

As a little girl, every day seemed to me to be cloudy. My mother told me the cloudy appearance was actually due to a problem with my eyesight. Her solution was simple; she would mix water and sugar and pour the drops into my eyes. She also prayed for me, and I can only attribute my recovery to her prayers. I have never had surgery on my eyes, but by the time I started school, I could see perfectly well. The Bible tells of mothers who prayed for their children and miraculous things happened. I am reminded of the Canaanite woman who asked Jesus to heal her daughter and Jesus had told her He was sent only to the lost sheep of Israel. This did not deter her at all. She wanted her daughter to get well at all costs (Matthew 15:21-28). I have asked medical professionals if the sugar and water mixture could have improved my sight, and they have assured me it would not; on the contrary this treatment might have further damaged my eyesight. The only explanation is that the Lord healed me. What I realized later is that I had had childhood cataracts. As I write this story, however, I do not have cataracts, I do not wear glasses, nor do I wear contact lenses. I can see pretty well for a woman my age.

By the time I started school, my parents had moved to the city of Gwelo (now called Gweru) where my father pastored a larger church. We lived in a roomy house on the church compound, which also included a spacious yard, gardens and a fruit

orchard, as well as a bookstore. My brothers, Njodzi and Benjamin, played with me in the yard, and we usually had the space to ourselves as our older siblings were either off working (several became teachers), or off at boarding school.

Like all of the black African children, Benjamin and I attended "Group B" schools, as only white and "mixed" kids could attend the "Group A" schools. B schools had large classes (45 or so students per class), while A schools kept class size around 20. B schools also lacked the more sophisticated resources (like lab equipment for a biology classroom) that would be found at a well-stocked A school. We walked about 25 minutes to and from school each day, making the round trip twice if we were taking part in after school activities like Girl Guides. On cold days, the ink in our pens often froze by the time we arrived at school. In the Domestic Science classroom, there was a wood stove used for teaching, and we took turns standing by the stove to thaw our pens and warm our freezing fingers.

In 1970, when I was seven years old, I started having nosebleeds on a daily basis. There were a number of known African remedies for nosebleed. For example, burning the quill of a porcupine and inhaling the smoke was thought to stop nosebleed; burning and inhaling dried elephant dung was another method (although elephant dung was not easy to find in my neighborhood); pouring cold water over the head was a third technique. My mother tried all of these, and the cold water cure sometimes actually helped. Most of the time the nose bleeds would eventually stop, but as time went on they worsened. One day my mom was concerned that I had lost too much blood and she suggested I lay my head down with my neck bent backwards to alleviate the bleeding. This position did indeed curb the nosebleed that day. I could feel the blood going down at the back of my throat. The following morning I wanted to lie down, so my mom brought out my mattress. As I got settled, I suddenly started to vomit profuse amounts of coagulated blood. I lost consciousness, and awoke in the Gweru General Hospital. My mother later informed me that I had been diagnosed with rheumatic fever.

While I was in the hospital, I didn't really think about God until a girl in the bed next to mine passed away. She had been hooked up to some of the same equipment as me. That night I felt too fearful to sleep. I was afraid that I would die, too. My mom tried to convince me that the other girl had not died, but had only been moved to another ward; when I suspected otherwise, however, my mom finally confessed the sad truth. After three weeks in the hospital, I was sent home with a list of new rules: I could not play sports. I should wear a hat whenever I was in the sun. I should take two penicillin pills every day for the rest of my life, a guideline I tended to forget. (After forgetting my pills a few too many times, I was switched to a once-a-month injection.) I had to try to avoid getting a sore throat (possibly the infection that led to developing rheumatic fever). I should avoid heavy lifting and any other stresses on the heart. The doctors said those stresses included bearing children, insisting it would be too risky.

The same year I was diagnosed with rheumatic fever, I also suffered from some of the more common childhood ailments, including a serious case of measles, becoming so weak that I could not walk on my own. Later that year, I developed mumps. While it was horrible to have those enlarged jaws and cheeks, the worst part was that, in my culture, the treatment for mumps was to wear dried corn meal husks around your neck. Despite the unusual treatment, I eventually recovered from every ailment except for the rheumatic heart disease, which I was told would be my partner for the rest of my life.

Still, my childhood was happy and, for the most part, it was normal, although my parents were very protective, and would not allow me to sleep away from home because they were afraid I would get sick. At school I was given special treatment. Besides not participating in any sport, I did not do any gardening with the other students. I sat in the classroom helping the teacher or starting homework assignments. I was faithfully attending my father's church, and singing in the choir, but I didn't think God could do anything about the rheumatic fever and didn't really think He cared either way.

Chapter 2
Wars and Rumors of Wars

R hodesia was named for the British explorer and businessman, Cecil Rhodes, who had come from the South African colony, crossing the Limpopo River in the 1890s to hunt for diamonds. Seeking mining rights from King Lobengula of Matabeleland, Rhodes claimed the area for the British crown. While many Britons migrated to the new colony, the white population never topped 5% of the total, yet the colony was consistently ruled by a white minority. Ian Douglas Smith was the last prime minister, serving from 1964-1979 (although Rhodesia was no longer recognized as an independent state by the international community at that time), and I recall him addressing the nation by radio when I was in high school, insisting that no black man would rule Rhodesia as long as he was alive. "Let me say it again. I don't believe in black majority rule ever in Rhodesia, not in a thousand years." As black Africans, we therefore understood that there were places we were not allowed to go (e.g., certain hospitals, restaurants, churches) because they

5

were for "whites only". I accepted that we were inferior to the white Rhodesians. It was not until I came to know Jesus as my Savior and I realized that I was created by God in His image, that I also came to believe that we are all equal in His sight.

My father always insisted that we watch the 8 pm news on TV. Prior to our buying a television set, we listened to the news on the radio. When I was in fourth or fifth grade, I began to hear rumors from my brothers. News was coming through from a Mozambique station. I was not allowed to listen to this station but I could hear adults talking. Most of the conversation was hushed. One day, though, people were marching and rioting in the streets. Then, suddenly, the bookstore on our compound was in flames. Everything in the store was burned and the store would never be rebuilt. The mobs did not touch our house or the church. It may have been tear gas that brought the quiet afterwards, but I was told the attack on the bookstore was nothing to worry about.

When I was in my final year of primary schooling (seventh grade in the Rhodesian system) my parents were transferred to yet another church, this one in a village. They let me remain in the city to complete my final year before high school, however, as I was already registered to take exams in this place. Changing schools could affect my high school placement.

Around the time of my parents' move, I started hearing about guerilla warfare. There was also talk about young men and women being recruited to go to Mozambique where they would train to fight for our freedom from British rule. I didn't know who was recruited, and a lot of the activity took place at night, so it was easy to become complacent until the day an armored vehicle in our village drove over a landmine, causing it to explode. My parents were concerned about a grandson and granddaughter who were staying with us in church housing in the village; I was visiting them during a school break and my parents urged our maid and me to carry the little ones on our backs and return them to the family homestead, over five miles away. We were advised to not use the main road where the landmine had exploded.

Freedom fighters, the ones who were fighting for our country's independence, and Rhodesian soldiers had been known to torture anyone they suspected of lying. My parents were trying to move us as far away as possible from potential danger. We ran the whole way to the family homestead and were relieved to arrive before dark as curfew was in place in most areas. I did fear for my parents, though, who had chosen to remain at the parsonage, but there was nothing I could do but wait to hear news. Thankfully, we heard from them the following day, and it turned out that both were still alive, and neither had been tortured. They told me they had prayed through the whole experience. They had been questioned along with others living near the school and church. A few of the others were taken into custody. Some were released after being questioned and beaten, but others did not come back.

We can learn a lot about people by the way they react to the stresses of war, and it was during the clash between Rhodesia's black majority and its white government that I discovered a lot about my family, my mother in particular. I knew that she had learned to manage on a limited budget when she and my father were in Bible School, finding creative ways to provide for her family, but I did not appreciate how much she knew until wartime. Due to a lack of supplies, many stores were closed and commodities were hard to find. That is when my mom started making her own soap, candles and jam, which neighbors would come and buy from her. She had already made clothes before the war, but began sewing shorts and shirts for little boys and dresses for little girls, also knitting or crocheting cardigans, hats, booties and receiving blankets. She continued to craft these items for the rest of her life. If anyone was unable to pay, or to barter or trade, my mother took on that person as a helper, giving her a chance to work off the cost of the soap, clothes, or whatever. Perhaps most importantly, my mother served as a midwife. Like the stores, most of the hospitals and clinics had also been shut down due to the war. Never charging for her services, my mother set aside a room where expectant mothers could come and stay until they gave birth. My mother

did not have any advanced medical equipment to help anyone with complications, but she prayed for all of her mothers and babies and God took care of them. I do not know the exact number of deliveries, except that it exceeded one hundred, and I am aware of only one mother and child who did not survive due to complications. The Lord truly blessed the work of her hands. The freedom fighters said my mother was doing her part in the war and so she was excused from the meetings they required everyone else to attend. My father likewise was exempt from these meetings, as he was known to pray for the freedom fighters. But none of this really registered with me at the time. I heard what they said and I heard my parents pray and I saw strange things happen, but somehow I did not see the hand of God.

My home was close to the main highway, Beitbridge Road, between Zimbabwe and South Africa. Convoys led by army vehicles, and trailed by more army vehicles, would often make their way along this road. Among the convoys would be cars bringing white people to do business in the capitol, making the trek to and from South Africa. More often than not, these cars made it safely through to Salisbury and back, but occasionally they would hit a landmine, causing considerable carnage, and resulting in the people living closest to the road being questioned and sometimes tortured. The soldiers would want to know who was responsible for the landmines on the main road. They did not leave until they were satisfied with the response. These were scary times. In the night, the freedom fighters would revisit to question the same people and, at times, if it could be established that they had said something to the Rhodesian Army, their lips would be brutally cut off. With the Rhodesian army loyal to the white minority government and the Freedom fighters working to rid Rhodesia of white rule, this time of war was hard on black people because they were caught between two opposing parties. I was one of them.

Chapter 3
Taking on the Armor of God

I was interviewed and accepted at the boarding high school, which three of my siblings had attended. By the time I actually started high school, however, the war was full-fledged, and no one knew if we would even be able to complete our secondary education.

During High School, I served as secretary of Scripture Union, the Christian group in the school. This group seemed like a natural outgrowth for me because of my connection with my parents' church. While I was committed to the group, however, I had no personal relationship with this God that we worshipped. I did not think anything else was required of me. I was a pretty good kid who only occasionally did some stupid things. When I was in my sophomore year, I started seeing a young man who did not go to the Scripture Union Group. I did not really care much for him but having a boyfriend made me feel more accepted by my friends, all of whom were seeing other young men.

One weekend, our Christian group hosted some guest speakers who travelled to different schools to share the good news about Jesus and encourage those who were believers already. As I listened to their message that weekend I found myself questioning my own beliefs and asking myself if I had any beliefs at all. One of the speakers read from Isaiah 64:6, "We have all become like one who is unclean, and all our righteous deeds are like a polluted garment" and Romans 3:23, "for all have sinned and fall short of the glory of God" (both ESV). Basically the message examined our righteousness in light of the holiness of God. It hit me there and then that, although I considered myself a "good" kid, I was a sinner. No one else could read my mind – but I realized that some of my thoughts were not good. There were times when I had even wished others dead because they had wronged me. As this speaker expounded on my goodness as compared to the righteousness of God, I knew I needed to do something. The problem was that I was already the secretary of the Christian group in the school; admitting that I just now realized I was a sinner who needed to be saved would be very embarrassing! But other things came to mind like the time I used tuition money as pocket money and lied to my parents that I needed money for something which was not true. I also recalled a time when I was quite small and I had stolen money from my parents' nightstand. Nobody had taught me to steal; it was something I was born with. I realized during that weekend that we are born with the desire to sin and that no one has to teach us to be sinful. What parents would ever tell their child to steal or to lie or to hide when they have done something wrong? A child does that on his or her own because we are born with sin and we cannot help but be selfish until something in us is changed by the Almighty God through Jesus. This reality dawned on me that weekend on the 12th of March, 1979 and when an altar call was made, I did not care who was watching. I went to the altar and I gave my life to the Lord – and my life has never been the same since! I am not saying that I am perfect. Far from it – but that is the day I admitted I was a sinner who needed to be saved

by Jesus Christ – and I started living and standing for something I believed in.

Because of my new life in Christ I began to see things in a new light. I saw how some "innocent" decisions can be hurtful and how sometimes you think you are such a blessing then realize that you are not. At this point, the young man I was dating did not want anything to do with me anymore. I was comfortable breaking off the relationship and dated a few others in my high school years but was not led to a serious relationship at that time. I had made the most important decision of my life; God gave me the tools not just to survive the war for my country's independence but also to equip me for trials I could never have imagined.

Chapter 4
From Rhodesia to Zimbabwe

During the war for Independence in Rhodesia, many boarding schools were closed because they became war zones, especially those in rural or remote parts of the country. My school remained open but we had our share of adventures. One week all of our teachers were arrested because they could not account for a number of students. Students and teachers alike suspected the missing students had gone to join the fight for freedom but never admitted to knowing that to be a fact. However, the male teachers were taken into custody. Since our school was left with only three female teachers, classes had to be cancelled for over a week. The teachers did not discuss the political situation; it was not allowed. Another time, the students had to ride in an army vehicle to get to the main road, so we could catch buses to go to our respective homes. I was unaware of the danger; I just enjoyed the thrill of riding in an armored vehicle. We eventually got to the main road without any incident although landmines had been common in that area.

Typically the freedom fighters would come by our school at night and ask us to do our part. Our part was to entertain them for that particular night. Specifically, we had to dance with them; they would borrow the teachers' stereos and bring them to the school dining room, where we would spend the whole night. Male and female students alike would assemble in the dining room until dawn and sometimes into the morning hours. From there we would just go to the dormitory and take showers and head for classes. As a result, we would be so tired that all we wanted to do was go to sleep. Sleep would be impossible. On the contrary, most of the time, around 8:00 am, the Rhodesian Armed Forces would come to our school, assemble us, and address us about the dangers of helping freedom fighters. Whenever they asked if we had seen the freedom fighters, we always insisted we had not. It was clear the soldiers did not believe us, and our teachers were sometimes reprimanded for students who had gone missing (including those who had gone to Mozambique to train to be soldiers). We experienced a number of other war related "adventures" and sometimes wondered if it would ever end. Most of us felt a sense of burden for the soldiers fighting for our freedom, knowing some were just a few years older; their lot was a lot harder than for those of us who were students. On the school front, the biggest problem was losing sleep and living in fear that one day we would be ambushed and killed all at once. Thankfully, it never happened.

I vividly recall another frightening night during the war. We had to observe a curfew at the school and remain inside our dormitories until morning. It was probably about 7 or 8 pm and we were just winding down, sharing stories. All of a sudden we heard voices outside asking us to come out and be educated on the reasons for the war and to do our part. We yelled that we were locked in and could not come out at that time. The freedom fighters outside did not accept that excuse and started yelling for us to jump through windows. Of course we were scared because our windows were over two feet from the floor yet quite a distance from the ground, which sloped downward from the building, and

the flower gardens below were covered in broken glass. The men were becoming so loud and agitated that some of the students started climbing up to the windows and tried to jump out. A few of us were lined up to jump when we heard gunfire, and then we quickly scampered under our beds. Then someone obtained keys and managed to unlock our dorms. We flocked out as quickly as we could. After we had settled down with a few men carrying different kinds of rifles, we were addressed by a very angry freedom fighter. He told us in no uncertain terms that we did not know what war was all about and we were still fooling around while others were doing their part in this fight. He acknowledged that school was important, because educated people would be needed once the war was over – but he implied that we were "spoiled brats" who didn't know how to sacrifice for the common good. We were then ordered to go back inside and in less than two minutes, we were to use only the two closest windows to exit the building. We ran back inside and tried to use the assigned windows to jump out at the assigned time. We were like animals trying to exit through a very narrow tunnel. Because of the rushing and the size of the windows, we were pushing each other – literally – through the windows. No one wanted to be the last one out. Most of us were injured on landing. Some sprained body parts, while others were badly cut or bruised. No one, however, said a word, though many of us were sore or bleeding. We all sat down in silence. Then we were addressed and taught a song about the revolution, about how this land had been ours, that foreign people had come in and taken our own land, pushing us away. We were then ordered to walk to a nearby church. Once we entered, one of the soldiers addressed us while another took a Bible; he said that it was white man's religion and he tore the Bible in front of us. We were all scared, though we remained in the church being "politicized", as they called it. It was very late by the time we were released and could return to our dormitory. This kind of roundup started to occur frequently, on one occasion keeping the students out as late as 5 am. Once again, by the time we went to bed, it was almost

time to get up and prepare to go to class. We were not excused from class. And as had happened in times past, we could hardly keep our eyes open when the Rhodesian soldiers showed up at our school. They made us all march outside our classrooms and started questioning us about the freedom fighters. As usual, nobody was willing to say a word. They surely suspected that the fighters had been around; what else would have accounted for our tired appearance? Events like these happened more times than I care to remember, but in no instance did anything fatal happen. God protected us and he protected our school. We did not have all the teachers we needed, but classes continued and the school struggled on. Meanwhile, the freedom fighters made sure we knew about their predecessors who had fought against the first British settlers a century earlier. Eventually the war would be over, the freedom fighters would win, and Rhodesia would be independent from British rule. The Lancaster agreement, formally ending the war and ushering in a new and independent nation, was eventually signed in December 1979.

To me, the saddest thing was that some freedom fighters were killed after the war. Many were stranded in remote areas, not knowing it was over. It took some of them a long time to find their way home.

Eventually, we were all encouraged to go and vote. I was still in high school the first time I voted. I did not yet have an ID, so the officials at the polling stations simply looked at us and asked us how old we were. They did not need much more than that, that first time. People came out in huge numbers and the ZANU-PF (Zimbabwe African National Union - Patriotic Front) won.

A temporary government led by black Africans had been organized under the name Zimbabwe-Rhodesia, in existence only from June-December 1979. Methodist Bishop Abel Muzorewa served as Prime Minister and educator Josiah Gumede as President during this six-month period. The following year, a new state was created, simply known as Zimbabwe, a name derived from a famous stone ruin, "The Great Zimbabwe" ["house of stones"],

a structure built without mortar that has stood for hundreds of years, serving on at least one occasion as a hiding place for the Shona when they and the Ndebele were at war. Major cities were also given Shona names, except in the southwest where Ndebele was prevalent. Salisbury, the capitol, became Harare (meaning roughly, "the town that never sleeps"). Our first independence celebration took place on April 18, 1980. Schools and businesses were closed and countrywide celebrations took place. Robert Mugabe, a jailed political activist and head of the ZANU party became the first prime minister of Zimbabwe and Canaan Banana, a pastor, its first president. By 1987, however, Mugabe was elected president. As I write this 30 years later, Robert Mugabe continues on as president of Zimbabwe, but the cries of celebration are a distant memory.

Chapter 5

We Become a Family

I wrote my O-Level examinations when I finished high school. After completing O-level exams, which were graded in the UK, one could go on to college and study to pursue careers like teaching and nursing or go on and study at the A-Level, which is to continue on until 12th grade. My brother Kudzai (Obadiah) had felt responsible for me and he and his wife determined that I should attend a teachers' college. On March 2, 1982, I started classes at a teaching college. I was not interested in teaching at the time, but when someone has done such a helpful thing for you, as my father reminded me, you should accept it and be grateful. I did just that. I started college late because the school year started in January; since I started on March 2, 1982, others had already made progress and I have to admit I was there with an unwilling heart. I was uncomfortable with public speaking, but felt compelled to attend and do my best.

During my years at teachers' college, I sensed a new feeling of hope in Zimbabwe. Now that the country was completely

free from British rule, President Mugabe had promised to improve the lives of Zimbabwe's black community. Along with the end of racial discrimination, we looked for a better economy, better schools, and more opportunities. I looked forward to being a part of it. I still felt less than enthusiastic about teacher training college. I was self-conscious and nervous speaking in front of an audience. As a result, my first teaching lesson garnered a grade of F. This is the only time I ever received an F in school and, while it depressed me, the poor grade also motivated me to do something about it. My professor called me to his office and asked me if I could tell him what had gone wrong with the lesson. The students were wondering what had happened to their teacher. Students are looking to their teacher to deliver a lesson, he explained, and to do that with confidence and joy. The pep talk encouraged me, it gave me a goal, and in my heart I pledged to be a teacher who could motivate and encourage my students in turn. I also felt bad about the failing grade, something I did not want to repeat. Public speaking did not suddenly become easy for me, but I gradually became more comfortable standing in front of the children and teaching them.

In college, I discovered several of the students I had known in high school were studying at the same college, including a young man I had dated. While we had not gone out for long and we had not had a very serious relationship, we continued to see each other in college. I knew from the scriptures, however, that I should not be unequally yoked with an unbeliever. I had to find a way to break off this relationship without sounding "holier than thou" and asked God to show me what to do. I soon learned that this man was seeing other women, including a married woman, a freshman, and a third woman claiming to be pregnant with this man's child.

After breaking off this relationship, I started dating a Christian young man, but we seemed to have nothing in common except our faith. While that may be the most important common ground, I still hoped that God had a partner for me, someone spe-

cial who would also share my goals and interests. That is the time I started praying for a life partner and I asked God to help me. I was still a fairly new Christian at this point and I dared to give God a fleece. I asked that He let no Christian man ask me out unless this man was the partner God had chosen for me. This man should be the first one to approach me after a long period of waiting. I prayed this prayer on the 1st of August, 1983. In December of the following year, I graduated from college.

Students were not required to pay tuition at the teachers' colleges in Zimbabwe. However, following graduation, they were required to put in at least two years teaching in a government school; a portion of their salary would then be deducted to "pay back" the government for the cost of their education. I was assigned to teach fourth grade in an all-black school in a city called Kwe Kwe. Before independence, the cost of schooling was beyond what many black Zimbabweans could afford. Now it was basically free for all. Best of all, for me, was that I discovered I had found my calling. I really enjoyed teaching, and I loved my students.

For two full years, not a single Christian man asked me out. I was about to give up hope, but in August of 1985, while I was participating in a Scripture Union camp, God answered my prayer. Martha, a friend and fellow camper, had been dating a man whose brother, Felix, led sports at the camp. She asked if I'd like to get to know Felix. He was very athletic and served as a soccer coach at the elementary school where he taught. He also led classes on the marimba, a wooden xylophone that originated in Africa. Felix was quiet and reserved, but quite good-looking and quite a big man. He was about seven years older than me, and I assumed he was married. As it turned out, he was single, and he was interested in me. If that was a coincidence, it was convincing, because even in my heart I knew this was the right man. We spent time getting to know one another, and one another's family and friends. Felix had a group of good friends, all single men, who referred to me as "Munhuwashe" (a person of God, or sent by God). I wonder if they realized I felt the same way about Felix. When

he proposed to me, I wanted to give him the answer right away, but he insisted I go and pray about it. All I did was go to God and thank Him for answering my prayers.

We became engaged in 1986. Up until our wedding I had continued to teach in Kwe Kwe, but during school breaks, we both served as counselors at a Scripture Union camp, this time working with young children. In preparation for our wedding, both of our families engaged the services of a go-between, a kind of moderator who represented the bride's or groom's family. In our case, he was my husband's best friend Charles and it was his responsibility to negotiate the bride price. My future husband was from the city and resented our village traditions, but he nevertheless complied with the price of ten cows, one cow to be presented to my mother, and nine to be presented in cash equivalents. The groom also traditionally provided all of the wedding clothes for the parents of the bride (that is, a suit, shirt, and shoes for my father and a dress and accessories for my mother). Special dishes for the bride's mother were also required. Meanwhile, I shopped in Botswana for fabric for my seven bridesmaids and ten flower girls.

Prior to the wedding, the bridal couple, their families, and all of their attendants needed to learn special dances to be performed at the receptions. Fortunately for us, Felix knew these dances and had actually served as a dance instructor for other wedding parties. It usually took weeks, however, to become proficient, so the rest of us spent our school vacations trying to get the hang of these dance movements. The movements were similar to a high-energy square dancing, led by a caller and requiring counting the number of steps out and back from a starting point. The music was upbeat, with singing in Shona, Zulu and Ndebele.

Our wedding took place on the morning of 29 August, 1987. Relatives had started to show up at my parents' house a week earlier, and we were responsible for providing room and board during their stay. The ceremony itself was just like an American ceremony. My wedding took place at the church where my father was serving. I walked down the church aisle on the arm of my un-

cle, who gave me away, since my father was officiating. A cake was served at the church. The reception(s) and all of the traditions, however, are uniquely African.

Following the ceremony, the wedding party and guests made the five-hour drive to the village where I had spent holidays as a little girl. There, on the fields surrounding the house my parents still owned, my family hosted a large reception. A cow had been slaughtered, and abundant servings of rice and chicken were served to the 300 assembled guests. Not all had received invitations; neighbors tend to just show up on these occasions. It was after the meal that the dancing began, and it went on long into the night. In the early morning hours, a special troupe came to perform Muchongoyo dancing, a traditional Shona-Ndou dance involving stomping and gestures and performed with a stick and shield, often to mark significant events. In addition to the professional dancers, wedding guests typically ask the bride to dance, offering cash for the privilege of dancing with her. It is traditional for the groom's family to object, at which time the guests start bidding on the bridesmaids – and they agree to dance. All monetary gifts are then presented to the bridal couple.

When it was finally time for bed, I slept in my parents' house and my husband stayed with his groomsmen, as tradition dictates. The following day, it was the bride's duty to make sure her husband has been given water to wash himself. Then her aunts and older sisters provide water for the bride, and give advice on how to care for her husband, mostly to be subservient. "He paid for you, now you belong to his family," they insisted. "Don't shame us by doing things you shouldn't."

In some cases, another reception follows, hosted by the groom's family, but we opted for a single reception, and moved on to the next round of negotiations. It was now the third evening following my wedding, and these negotiations involved only my aunt (a family member who had been chosen because she represented my values) and Felix's uncle and the uncle's wife. My aunt sought further bride payments prior to giving me to the Chidzeros

21

as Felix's bride. Normally, they negotiate every item (such as the spoon I will use to stir the pot of stew or an item of clothing I will bring or surrender), but the Chidzeros kindly offered to negotiate everything as a "group purchase". With the business completed, I spent the night with my aunt in order to receive further counsel, while Felix spent another night alone.

Finally, on the next day, my aunt returned to her home after having formally given me to my husband's family. Felix and I left for the Eastern Highlands where we had booked a hotel for our honeymoon. You have to be a very patient man if you are going to marry an African woman!

Two months after our wedding, I was expecting our first child. While I was miserably ill for most of the pregnancy, I was most concerned that the heart problem I'd had since childhood could endanger my own health or that of my unborn child. In my culture, we have a special ceremony to prepare for the birth of the first child in the family. The ceremony is held at the home of the new mother's family and takes place about the seventh month; after the ceremony, the new mother usually moves back home, staying with her mother through the birth and an additional two or three months, to learn how to care for her baby. Because of my precarious health, however, I was instructed to remain in Harare, where we now resided, close to a main hospital and to my doctor, and my mother planned to move to our home instead.

At the end of seven months, before the ceremony took place, my water broke, and I was placed on strict bed rest at the Avenues Clinic in Harare. Felix took a bus to my parents' village to let them know I was in the hospital and could not join them for the ceremony.

During his absence, I was discharged, and Felix's sister drove me home. The next morning, my labor pains began. Esther, a young woman who lived with us, was charged with finding the pastor when I started labor, as he owned a car and had offered to drive us to the hospital. Esther ran to the pastor's house but he was not home. She then searched for one of the church dea-

cons who had a car, but he was nowhere to be found, either. A neighbor suggested we call for an ambulance. But it turned out the ambulance dispatcher had received so many false alarms that he required we make the request in person. So Esther ran to the nearest police station, and ended up returning by ambulance. I made it to the hospital, and at 1:15 pm, gave birth to a premature baby son named Simbarashe ("power of God"). He weighed just over 2 kilograms (4.4 lbs.) and was placed in an incubator. I came down with a fever; all of the joints in my body were burning and I could not sleep. Finally, Felix arrived, and he stayed with me until well after midnight. By morning my life was out of danger and I fell asleep. Still, I could not have taken care of my son in that condition and was thankful to God that he was safely sleeping in an incubator that first night.

By his fifth month my tiny son had grown remarkably, and had caught up with his age mates. My husband and I were a very happy mother and father.

Chapter 6
"Trust in God"

When Simba was about two and a half we started to yearn for another child, even though I still had concerns about being ill during or after giving birth. By October 1990, I was pregnant. This time, I was amazed at my good health throughout the pregnancy. Although I still took my heart injection, I suffered no morning sickness and felt healthy through and through. On July 20 of 1991, we were blessed with a healthy baby girl. We named her Vimbainashe which means "trust in God". This time around, the labor lasted only an hour and I did not become sick at any time, either during or after labor. My daughter grew fast and my son continued to thrive. By nine months Vimbainashe was walking, though she had yet to cut a single tooth. She never needed to see a doctor for any illness, and if she had a cold, which was rare, it would clear quickly. After she turned a year old, however, Vimbainashe started crying at night; Felix and I would wake up and take turns taking care of

her. After a few months, her ankles began to swell. I took her to several doctors and I was given many different diagnoses, but none of them ended up being correct. My daughter continued to cry; her face, arms, and other areas began to swell. One day I took her to a new doctor who had a surgery close to where we lived. When he asked for a urine sample, I explained that it would be difficult since my daughter hardly wet her nappy. The doctor then suspected he knew what was wrong with my daughter. He gave us a urine bag to take home. Eventually she urinated and I took the samples to a lab for analysis. The results were as the doctor had suspected. Vimbainashe had a kidney infection. He referred us back to our pediatrician with those results.

Vimbainashe was sent to the hospital where she received medication since she was too young to undergo dialysis. At first she seemed to recover, but then the fluid started gathering in her arms and feet again. This cycle continued for about 10 months. She would go into the hospital, get better, we would come home, and after a while it would happen again. On one of those occasions, while we were in the hospital, my little girl suffered a stroke. As I stayed with her in the hospital, I thought that she would die since she was breathing heavily and making loud noises. She was transferred to the Intensive Care Unit where she stayed for a week. The doctor gave me the heartbreaking news that the stroke had deprived her of her senses. She could not feel, she could not see, she could not hear. Five days later, however, she regained her hearing and sense of touch. She was discharged from the Intensive Care Unit to the regular children's ward where she was administered medicine for high blood pressure, and she continued to improve.

One day, I was feeding her from a blue plastic cup while talking to another mother. I realized Vimbainashe was following the direction of the cup with her eyes. I knew that she could see; my baby could see again. I was ecstatic! She had now regained her senses and seemed recovered but then, very suddenly, this little girl who had learned to walk at nine months could suddenly no longer stand. She returned to the hospital one more time, al-

though the doctor felt pretty certain her kidneys were now functioning normally.

Prior to Vimbainashe's illness, I had continued teaching, along with my husband, who was also a teacher. I had started a Scripture Union group at my school. We gathered after the school day for singing, scripture memory, and to hear special speakers. Felix and I spent many school breaks at Scripture Union Camps. Our children delighted in being outdoors and spending extra time with us.

Then one day, Paul Makanyanga, an administrator for Scripture Union, came to our house to talk to my husband about working for Scripture Union full time. We prayed about it and came to believe that God was calling him to this work. Thus, in 1992, Felix left his teaching position to join Scripture Union full time. I continued to teach and we worked side by side during school vacations. Felix loved this work although it often took him away from home, which was difficult during the period when Vimbainashe was in and out of the hospital.

On the day before she was to be discharged, Vimbainashe suffered a seizure and the doctor decided to give her a blood transfusion. The seizure was a reaction to the lengthy fight against Nephrotic syndrome and the doctor felt her blood needed a boost. Struggling to find a vein, they opted to give her a transfusion through a vein in the head. The transfusion went well for the first two units and we were advised to return home since she had had no adverse reaction to the blood she had received so far. With one more unit to go, we went on home.

The next morning was a Sunday and my husband did what he always did. He took me to the hospital and, after praying in the chapel for a while, he would go either to work or to church. After he left me in the room, he went to the chapel to pray. I went to see Vimbainashe, and as I picked her up I could see she had brownish stuff on her mouth. I wiped it and was about to feed her when her head went limp in my hands. I screamed and a nurse came running. They started calling for a code something and running

around. One of the other nurses on duty pulled me away into the nurses' station while they searched for my husband. After Felix arrived, a nurse reported that our daughter was stable and the doctor was on his way. She had been moved to the ICU, where we were now escorted. We were startled to see Vimbainashe tethered to a cluster of intravenous tubes. I couldn't understand. My daughter was supposed to be discharged that day. Now, every time she breathed, blood gushed from her nose and mouth. I couldn't stop crying. The doctor finally came to tell us that they had failed to monitor her blood pressure during the last stage of the transfusion. Too much blood had been administered, and the pulmonary artery had burst. Nothing could be done except to administer plasma in the hope that it would stop the internal bleeding. What the doctor did not tell me (but did tell my husband) was that he really had no solution to this problem. Essentially, we were waiting for my daughter to bleed to death. That was the longest and hardest day I have ever had to endure. My daughter would hold onto my finger and, as I squeezed her hand, she would do the same, but as the day went on the hold got weaker and her skin grew pale.

My mother-in-law came to the hospital, bringing food, but I was unable to eat. "You must eat," she advised. "If the child lives, you will need strength to take care of her. If she dies, you will need strength to grieve for your daughter. Either Way, you will need strength." I forced myself to eat.

Around 4:30 pm, I watched the monitor stop drawing the regular zigzags of a beating heart and start to register a straight line and then a downward slope. I couldn't take my eyes off the monitor. In the meantime, my husband was trying to reach friends and relatives. Our pastor had already visited and had solicited prayer from the church. My parents had gotten word that the baby was worse, and they were en route. I was unaware of what was going on; I could only gaze at the monitor and feel numb. Meanwhile Felix had returned; he suggested I go downstairs to the lobby, where my brother and his wife awaited news, and let them know

how the baby was faring. I hadn't gotten far when I was called to the doctor's office to sign forms allowing him to operate on our daughter. While that didn't make any sense, the doctor had decided that there was nothing to lose and an operation might save her. This seemed like too much, and my legs suddenly became very heavy. I had to drag myself to the elevator, then to the Intensive Care Unit on the fifth floor. When we got to my daughter's bedside, I was very relieved to see that she had fallen asleep and appeared to be fine, as she was not connected to tubes anymore. My first reaction was to go and pick her up. In my mind I thought she had been miraculously healed.

As I moved closer, however, my husband and his friend Charles pulled me back. Felix said, "She is gone." I cried out in anguish and then everything in the room seemed to fade away. When I revived, we were in a darkish room and I was told my daughter was lying there right on my side. I saw the covering and began to weep. This was not happening. How could this healthy, happy little girl be gone? How could God take our miracle away from me? No matter how much I tried to reason it out, the reality was there and there was nothing I could do to deny it. My heart felt shattered; so did my world.

By evening everyone was gathered at my mother-in-law's house for a funeral gathering for my daughter. I have no recollection of how and when I got there, but in no time, friends and family had come and they were crying along with me. Someone brought Simba to me; I hugged him tight and cried for his loss. I did not see my husband again until after the burial. By late evening both my parents had arrived. My father, as well as my pastor, preached at the funeral. I appreciated my mother's presence; she had come to comfort me the best way she knew how. She had never lost a child but I knew her heart was crying for me. This was the 14th of November in the year 1993. My daughter was buried a few days later, and I was taken to my own house. All through the time I spent at my mother-in-law's house, I had been surrounded by family and friends and they had stayed the whole time and sang

Gospel songs and prayed until the day my daughter was laid to rest. Her burial was very hard for me, but the most difficult time was when I returned home and it started to rain. That is when I felt like the negligent parent who left her child out in the rain and mud while I was in a nice warm bed. I could not sleep, although eventually exhaustion won and sleep stole me.

The coming days continued to feel empty and sad. I wanted to press a reverse button and discover it had all been a mistake or I had been dreaming. In a few weeks, school was out for Christmas break and my husband took me home to be with my parents. My son was there, but it was just so hard to focus on anything except my own loss and grief. Little did I know that my parents, who only wanted to comfort me, were about to face even greater challenges.

Chapter 7

A Sad Christmas Observance

A s soon as I saw my parents, I realized that my father
was not well. When he had spoken at my daughter's
funeral, he did not seem ill. Now, however, he seemed
to think the Lord was calling him home. Thus, even as I came
seeking comfort in my loss, my father was talking about his own
"impending" death. My mother did not want to hear my father's
words, so I became my father's "sounding board", and listened to
him talk about what he wanted done after his death. I was still
in a state of shock and could hardly believe what was happening.
Everyone viewed my father as an invincible man of God who
had enjoyed good health most of our lives. He told me that he'd
started writing a memoir; since he could not continue, he wanted
me to finish writing while he dictated. As an obedient African
daughter, I did not question his motives. I sensed that my mother
was in denial, running away from my father's words, but I did not
know what else to do.

Transcribing my father's memories kept me busy, as I focused on his story, and I had little time to myself to think about the daughter whom I had just buried. I realized I had some unfinished business, but I lacked the emotional energy to deal both with my father and the feelings I had for my daughter. So I just focused on what I was asked to do. I turned off my feelings for a while. I felt in my heart that my father knew what he was talking about, but I could not reconcile that with the fact that he did not appear to have a fatal condition.

After my father became ill, any time my mother asked him to resolve an issue, he would advise her to address it herself, pointing out that she would have to be in charge when he was gone. The following month was December and it found me in a trance-like state. I continued to transcribe the words my father asked me to write. My mother continued to try to engage him in other areas, but it was not an easy task. As we neared Christmas, my father seemed to be getting worse. He was unable to eat and seemed uncomfortable. He could not do a lot of things he loved doing in the past.

As was our family tradition, most of my brothers and sisters came to the village with their families just before Christmas. Usually they would stay just till the start of the New Year. This year, my siblings had a chance to see for themselves that our father was ill. None of them believed he would die, though. Normally, my mother was the sickly one in our family. Most of the men folk would take some time out after meals and go out for drinks at the nearest shopping center. My husband, who did not drink, opted to stay at home with me. As much as I appreciated his presence, however, I could not share what was going on inside me. I did not know how to put into words the turmoil in my heart and soul. On Christmas morning, our custom was to bathe, don new clothes, eat a hearty breakfast, and share a time of devotions, led by my father. Afterwards, family members were free to go where they wanted to spend the day, although typically the ladies stayed around to prepare the big feast for everyone. We usually had a

goat or other animal slaughtered, along with some chickens. This year my father was unable to get out of bed, and therefore unable to lead Christmas day devotions. The next day, however, he did manage to get up and, even though his legs were swollen, he stood and led devotions. Afterward, he called on my oldest brother, Jacob, and read to him the words Moses spoke as a farewell to Joshua. Then he began to cry, not because he was afraid to die, but because he feared a long illness. As he struggled to stand on his very swollen feet, I struggled with my own pain, as the thought of the death of my daughter seemed to merge into a nightmare that now included my father. I still wondered if, at some point, someone would wake me up and tell me everything was okay. My father was later taken to a hospital in a nearby town, where my second oldest brother made provision for him as he was managing director of a mining town near the hospital. There my father was diagnosed with prostate cancer and sent to a larger hospital, Saint Anne's, in Harare.

During this time, I accompanied my parents everywhere. At Saint Anne's my father was scheduled for surgery. Although the operation was successful and he initially seemed to be making a full recovery, he later relapsed and died on January 18, 1994, two months and 4 days after my daughter had died. The world suddenly became a very painful place; as I, along with my mother and siblings, each struggled with our own grief.

I remember very little from the events following my father's death, as everything seemed a blur of activity. My family tried to keep my husband busy as is our custom. The nightmare just seemed to be growing bleaker. Everything around me felt black; there were no grays. My husband's truck carried my father's casket. I rode in the truck along with my mother and my mother-in-law. My father was buried within two days of our return home. Thousands of mourners showed up for his funeral. I have never in my life seen so many people at one funeral - and they all came from different churches and denominations. The service was such a tribute to my father's ministry over the years. Yet I felt all

alone. It was hard to think that the man who had preached at my daughter's funeral was gone. I just couldn't process the reality that both my daughter and now my father were gone. Even though my father had anticipated his own death, it didn't make the loss any easier to bear. My pastor's wife and my friend Emma had reached out to support me, but I wondered who would understand how I felt after losing my child and my father. My mother had never lost a child but she was now struggling over the loss of her husband. It did not occur to me that she would understand my feelings, so I just struggled by myself.

In time, though, I felt a sense of comfort over my father's death. I knew he was with the Lord and he was no longer suffering from the pain and other symptoms that had surfaced over Christmas. But even as I made peace with my father's passing, I just couldn't get over the grief of losing my daughter. I couldn't function. I made an appointment with my pastor and asked him what to do with all this pain. He admitted he did not have a clear-cut answer for me, but he did give me a verse from the Bible. Job 23:10 says, "He knows the way I take; after He has tested me I will come forth as gold." I did not care about coming out as gold, however; all I wanted was to come out of that overwhelming grief. It felt like a huge obstruction that barred me even from the joy of being with my son, Simba. I just ached for my daughter. Of course the pain eventually did grow less intense and I was even able to sleep at night. Still, every time I saw a little girl who would have been my daughter's age, I thought about her and the pain would begin again. I felt that a brook had just run dry on us - but the Lord would be our source of healing.

Chapter 8

A New Home

After my husband had been working for Scripture Union for some time, the organization asked him to consider traveling to the United States to get a Bible degree, and thereby also gain exposure to people from different cultures. On the advice of a good friend, Terry King, an American who was serving as an evangelical missionary in Zimbabwe, Felix applied to Rhode Island Bible Institute[1]. Scripture Union did not have funding to send Simba and me, so we decided, after considerable deliberation and prayer, that Felix would go first (in August 1996), while Simba and I would follow in December. By then, we hoped airfare would be available as well as housing for all of us on campus.

December seemed like a long way off, and I shed a lot of tears the day Felix left, but the Lord gave me comfort during those days and Simba was good company, always cheerful. Towards the end of the year, I resigned from my teaching position in preparation for our move to the United States, only to discover that

we still did not have enough funds for airfare and my husband's Bible College was advising international students not to have their families join them. Felix also warned me that students had little opportunity to work off campus due to the demands of schoolwork and the requirement that each student devote 35 hours each week to campus maintenance as a work-study arrangement. Furthermore, campus accommodation for families was scarce. But the Lord provided for me in Zimbabwe. During Felix's absence, a young woman stayed with us, serving both as a companion for me and as an occasional babysitter for Simba. Nancy was a Godsend. I remember waking in the middle of the night to find her on her knees praying for my family. I really needed those prayers, as I was starting to lose hope of ever seeing my husband again.

During our separation, Felix faced challenges as well, as he acclimated to new academic and social structures and dealt with loneliness and concern for the family waiting for him in Zimbabwe. It was difficult to understand why the school appeared to discriminate against families in this way. We felt that God was calling both of us; we had anticipated studying together and working together, as the Lord opened doors for us.

God provided help for us in the person of Mrs. McCullough, a white Zimbabwean woman who was a Scripture Union associate; she organized a concert to raise funds for my son and I. Another friend, Dunmore, and his wife suggested I write letters to my siblings, seeking some support. Although I was reluctant to ask, they did provide us with enough funding that we could finally buy our tickets! Lovemore, a Zimbabwean family friend who was then working for the United Nations in New York, provided the necessary letters of invitation, welcoming us to stay with him while my husband was in school. Of course our plan was to live with Felix at school in Rhode Island, but we were required to verify that we had a sponsor who could provide housing for us, lest we become a burden on the US government. We were then able to apply for visas and, finally, on the 8th of May 1997 (my husband's birthday), we arrived in New York!

We were thrilled to have our family reunited. We spent most of our summer in New York and in Hartford, Connecticut, where we volunteered at a Salvation Army camp. Felix invited a fellow student to join us; Towera had come from Zambia to study at RIBI. The two of us became fast friends and we all appreciated the opportunity to work with these children who came to camp from very broken homes and difficult backgrounds. Meanwhile I had been accepted by Felix's college and was overjoyed when they accepted me. We looked forward to being together as a family again. Simba was now nine years old and we registered him at the local public school. Soon after we settled in, he was featured on a TV commercial for nearby Roger Williams Zoo; now we really felt part of a community!

The college provided a small apartment with a living room, bedroom, small kitchen, and a bathroom. Our son slept in the living/dining room. God continued to provide for us in so many ways: My student visa application was approved. A friend helped with living expenses. The school had a "blessing table", where students could find nice second-hand clothing. We were able to get meals from the college dining room. We never went to bed hungry; that is for sure. I was able to generate a little income through babysitting and housecleaning jobs and my husband did yard work. The college proved to be a great place for us spiritually. By December 1997, we had settled into college life, and felt blessed to be in college together and to have Simba with us.

But that same month, just before the Christmas break, I began to feel sick and sought out a local doctor. He did not bill me for the examination (he was a Roman Catholic doctor), which was another huge blessing. He confirmed that I was pregnant and that the baby was due in August of the following year. I had been warned about the risks of having children when I was diagnosed with rheumatic heart disease, but even though the stress of a pregnancy could compromise my health, I was thankful for this news. I felt confident in the doctor, who would treat me for a high-risk pregnancy, but my ultimate confidence was in the Lord.

We visited friends in New York over the holidays. I had decided to break the news to my mother shortly after Christmas. After the losses we had suffered in the last three years, I knew my mother would be happy about the prospect of new life. On the 29th of December, however, my niece called from England with some terrible news. After suffering a massive stroke on the 26th of December, my mother had died. She was to be buried on December 29th, the very day my niece called. My family had been trying to locate me since the day of the stroke, but had been unable to reach me while I was in New York. Finally a campus friend spoke to my niece and provided my contact information. When I left for the USA, my mother was a robust 76-year-old. The stroke took everyone by surprise, even those family members who lived in the same house.

For some reason just before I got the news about my mother's death, I listened to "I Remember Mama" by Shirley Caesar, and so it became a very significant song for me. Additionally, I had had a dream, in which I was swimming in water that turned black and blinding. Perhaps this subliminal message helped prepare me for the loss of my mother.

Still, my mother and I had been very close and it would be a long time before I could absorb the fact that she was gone. I had so looked forward to sharing my news, and wondered if anyone else would care about this new life. God is good, however, and He gave me the best of friends: Towera, our fellow student from Zambia, who was very supportive; Lovemore, my husband's best friend; Marjorie and Patty, two dear sisters in Christ, who were great comforters and encouragers. They prayed with and for me.

These good friends cared deeply for my husband and me, but as I grieved over my mother, I began to agonize that this baby would die like my little daughter. I should have left the worries with God, as we are reminded to "cast all your anxieties on Him for He cares for you" (1 Peter 5:7). Instead, I kept pondering the risks; I didn't want to die and I was concerned I would have a child with serious health defects. I was already 35 and my husband was about 42. My husband was a student and we were living in a coun-

try that was new to us; suddenly the timing seemed the worst ever.

To top it all, we were living on campus in a cramped, two-room apartment with very little income and I worried how we would provide this baby with even the most basic needs. Neither Felix nor I was employed, other than the few dollars we picked up from the occasional babysitting and yard work. We were in a foreign country and my faith had hit rock bottom, but God knew that as well. I should have been happy about the baby, but felt I could not talk to anyone who would understand what I felt at the loss of my mother, and the concerns over my baby. But God's timing – and his provision – never fail.

Chapter 9

Watching God Provide all I Needed

What should I do to mark the loss of my mother? I was afraid that the 20-plus hour trip by plane to Zimbabwe, especially in my first trimester, could jeopardize the baby's health. Secondly, we had no funds for such a trip. And finally, what use would it be for me to return to Zimbabwe? My mother was already buried. While I could rationalize not going home – and did not end up going – I still fell into a state of despair, knowing that there was nothing I could have done to prevent my mother's death, while facing the reality that I would not see her again this side of heaven.

Once again, I felt I was just going through the motions of life. I would read my Bible and pray, but often prayed mechanically or did not absorb what I was reading. I even stopped caring whether or not I would actually give birth to this child. But God is faithful, and I thank Him for friends and family and especially for brothers and sisters in Christ, who will pray with you when

you cannot pray. It is by the help of the Holy Spirit that we are able to pray, Gal 4:6, "And because you are sons, God has sent forth the Spirit of His Son into your hearts, crying out, 'Abba, Father!'" (Gal. 4:6) and "Likewise the Spirit also helps us in our weaknesses. For we do not know what we should pray for as we ought, but the Spirit Himself makes intercession for us with groaning which cannot be uttered" (Rom 8:26).

After Christmas break, we returned to campus, but I found it hard to get motivated to do schoolwork. Ironically, I was enrolled in a class on the book of Thessalonians, a book in which Paul specifically reminds the Thessalonians about the hope we have in Jesus Christ. I had little hope that we'd have the means to support this baby. We often scanned the "blessing table" to find good, used clothes, but there was rarely clothing for young boys like Simba or for babies.

Neither my husband nor I owned a computer, but I was usually able to borrow a laptop from another student when one of us needed to submit a hard copy of a paper. On one occasion, I recall trying to type a paper even though I felt quite ill with morning sickness. I ended up getting sick all over my jacket, and the foul smell attracted the attention of one of the students' advisors, as I was making my way back to my apartment. This wise elderly woman, who also oversaw hospitality on campus, asked after me, advised me to clean up, and to then return to see her. Sister Marjorie was pleased to relate how she knew of my arrival in the USA from Africa. She told me that she noted a sparkle in my husband's eyes when my son and I arrived. She had never met me but knew I was there because my husband had become a happy man. She wanted to know what was troubling me. I shared my dual concerns about the pregnancy and about losing my mom. When I told her my mother had been a believer, she reassured me that my mother had entered the rest she deserved and that the Lord knew what was going to happen; He did not want me to continue to be overwhelmed with grief over my mother but to now focus on the baby. We continued to meet and to pray together.

This sister in Christ, Marjorie, did not condemn me for my lack of faith; instead, she gave me something to look forward to. God had sent someone who was prepared to stand with me and pray with me. Even though I still faced health risks and financial hardship, she helped me trust God to provide what I was lacking. The more we prayed, the more I sensed these issues could be resolved. Suddenly I was looking forward to this baby. By the time I reached the sixth month of my pregnancy, I actually started to consider names for this baby.

God provided another wonderful friend who became my "American mother": Arline, who attended Foursquare Gospel Church in Providence, where Felix and I served as interns. She took me under her wing and drove me to doctors' visits and other errands. One day she took me for an ultrasound scan, joining me in the examining room, and we saw a baby whose hands were lifted up as if in worship. My American mom cried out with excitement, "Your baby is praising God already."

Marjorie and Patty, along with Towera and Lovemore, provided the love, comfort and encouragement I needed to get through this period. I finally felt ready to welcome this little child. As we continued to pray together, the prayers seemed to impact our family; we felt happier, reassured. We all looked forward to this new addition, and after the ultrasound, I knew the baby would be a girl.

I also began to think about seeing my mother again one day. I had only seen her death as one more precious life the Lord had taken from me, but now I thought of her as one more treasure I will see when I get home to heaven.

But we continued to fret about our finances. I had a regular babysitting job for a little girl whose parents were psychologists but now my doctor was advising I get more rest. The only income we had was from this babysitting job and occasional seasonal yard work. The Kings, the missionary couple who had served in Zimbabwe occasionally sent us checks; they were graduates of RIBI, and it was they who had recommended that my husband and I apply to their alma mater.

But of course the Lord continued to prove that He is faithful. We always had enough to eat and my "mom" Arline continued to get me to medical appointments. But our school held to a strict dress code and I was struggling to find a skirt that would fit around my expanding waist. Thankfully, the school bowed to student pressure and instituted a new dress code about that time. We were now allowed to dress as we would for ministry, which gave me a lot more leeway in finding appropriate clothes that would accommodate my changing figure.

I was thankful that God was giving me another girl -- if only I could get the negative thoughts out of my mind. Sometimes I would remember, as if it had happened the day before, the agony of losing my first daughter, and I could not sleep. It would take time to tell my troubled soul that the God who had brought us this far had not done that so as to abandon us, but to give us a hope and a future. On some of these occasions, I would go to sleep early and wake up to find my husband studying in the middle of the night. Some nights he did not sleep at all. He began suffering from frequent headaches, but would just take over-the-counter medication and continue with his schoolwork.

I had told our pastor's wife at Foursquare Gospel Church, where we interned, that we were expecting a baby girl. The church received many donations of used clothing, but didn't have any items for baby girls in their closet – so we began praying for donations. By the end of June (two months before the baby was due), several large boxes of girls' clothes had been donated. We did not open these boxes since I did not have time, with classes and all other responsibilities.

Towera continued to be a blessing to me. She cleaned my apartment a couple of times each week and – even more importantly – took time to pray for me. Thank God for these Marthas who also have a Mary spirit. One might think that all of this support from my fellow believers would banish my fears, but that was not the case. If I were not worrying about the birth itself, I fretted about the baby's health or the size of our tiny apartment. I have

since realized that if I start worrying about one issue or another, the enemy shows me more things I need to worry about. It was a good thing I was surrounded by so much support, as these thoughts intruded only when I could not sleep.

My baby's due date was August second, but I awoke with labor pains on July 24th. Early the next morning, we were blessed with a healthy baby girl. Hallelujah! Thank you Lord. We had already decided on a name because I felt the Lord's Shekinah[1] glory had seen me through this pregnancy. This "unplanned baby" was born 5 days after her late sister's birthday. That could have inspired fear, but instead I felt God had restored to us the joy that death had taken from my family.

One item we had lacked was a car seat, but again God proved faithful. By the time we were released from the hospital with our little bundle of joy, we had been given a seat for her. On that same day, I received a surprise. Friends at the college had planned a baby shower for my little girl. Although baby showers are common in Zimbabwe, especially in the cities, I did not expect this outpouring of love and gifts. I cried and laughed as I opened one package after another, to find all the clothes we would need for the first few months.

Someone had also blessed us with a baby stroller. As if that hadn't been enough of a blessing, the ladies at the Foursquare Gospel Church had also planned a baby shower for us! I received more new clothes for my little girl and - would you believe it? - another baby stroller, so now I had two and I was looking to bless someone else. After the shower, the pastor's wife gave me the boxes of hand-me-down girls' clothes we had prayed for. We found everything from baby clothes up to clothes for a ten year old. And to think that I had despaired of having the means to provide all

---

[1]*The word Shekinah is from the Hebrew "shekinot" where God is said to "settle in" or "dwell with." This word refers to that place where God is dwelling, settling or where His Divine Presence is.*

of the clothes and other necessities needed to raise my baby! To top it all, God sent a blessing in the form of a pediatrician. He was already my son's doctor and he was the best one for my daughter. I have yet to meet another doctor like him.

How great is our God. Like my first two children, my daughter became and remains a joy to my life. It's very rare to find her unhappy. One of my friends whose own daughter is a friend of Shekinah gave her the nickname "Bubbles" for her joyful personality. Simba, being ten years older, was an eager and helpful babysitter as I did housework and homework.

Chapter 10
Back to Africa: Part 1

My husband was a conscientious student, maintaining a 4.0 GPA in all of his classes. In 1999 it became apparent that he would be able to graduate in three rather than the usual four years. We had determined that I would earn a one-year certificate and then we would both apply to Gordon College, with Felix continuing into a Master's Program and me completing my Bible Degree. At the last minute, however, we got cold feet, feeling it would make more sense for us to stay in one place and then move on to graduate school together after I had completed my bachelor's degree in Bible School. Thus, in May 1999, when our daughter was just 10 months old, my husband graduated with High Honors. Friends came from New York and all the way from Harare. Our two pastors from Zimbabwe, as well as a gospel singer friend, showed up. What a time of celebration it was!

The following August, we got the sad news that my sister-in-law had died, following an illness. She was the wife of Jephta

(Njodzi), the seventh born, and I especially grieved for their little girl who was just seven years old.

Back at school that fall, my days were divided between the demands of schoolwork and running after my now one-year-old daughter. Occasionally, Shekinah would say a new word or take a few steps on her own, and I wished I could share these milestones with my mother. But I'd keep these thoughts in check, count my blessings, and be thankful for God's goodness to me. One blessing was a larger apartment in a small two-story building on campus. We lived upstairs and our unit encompassed two bedrooms along with a very large living room and dining room. Our first-floor neighbors were Gloria and Jabez Rapaka, who went on to study at Regent University, and from there to start outreach ministries in Haiti and in India. Our little building was referred to as the White House because of the white shingles covering the structure.

It became our custom to celebrate Christmas and the New Year, as well as nearly every school holiday, in New York. Lovemore, our friend and benefactor, was our host, and we were very blessed to have a place that served as a retreat for us when we were away from campus. Now that our daughter was about a year and a half, I stopped worrying so much about whether or not she would survive. God gave me a peace about this child. He was my Peace and his peace passes all understanding.

Our son was thriving in school and we were content in our ministry, yet I struggled to put closure on my mother's death. Since we had so little income, I could not consider flying home. But in December I heard that my brother, who had recently lost his wife, was very sick and his prognosis was not good.

Besides facing the anguish of losing yet another beloved family member, I knew Jephta was not saved and that he thought all that "garbage" about receiving Christ was a form of brainwashing. He had even urged our parents to sell the guitar on which I played Gospel songs. Eventually I sold it just to appease him. I appealed to the Lord to please do something to change Jephta's heart. Eventually he was hospitalized and slipped into a coma. My

classmates prayed for him – and he actually regained consciousness; in fact, he was alert enough to receive Christ as His Lord and Savior. The following month, on February 14, 2000, God called my brother home, at the age of 44. I grieved both for him and his daughter, Svitsai, who now had neither mother nor father. Obadiah (Kudzai), my second oldest brother, stepped in to care for her. Obviously I could not go home. As I was grieving, a friend and classmate named Jackie came along beside me, crying, and then praying with me. She assured me that the Lord was seeing my grief, and comforted me with a passage she said the Lord had given her for me,

> *"Fear not, for you will not be ashamed;*
> *be not confounded, for you will not be disgraced;*
> *for you will forget the shame of your youth,*
> *and the reproach of your widowhood you will remember no*
> *more. (Isaiah 54:4-5)*

I felt comforted, although I was puzzled that she had said I was a widow, which was not the case. True, my husband worked a lot of hours and double shifts when possible at his security job, but I was not widowed. I shared this passage with my husband and he sought out Jackie on a day off, asking her to stop referring to me as a widow, as it was distressing to me. Felix worked long hours, as this was our only source of income, but he did love me and looked forward to the day when he'd have more time to devote to his family.

The following summer, I was preparing to travel to Africa, bringing little Shekinah with me. We would first head to New Jersey, where "Uncle" Lovemore now resided, and we would fly out of Newark. I couldn't wait to show my family this beautiful girl whom God had blessed us with, but I also yearned to see where my mother, sister-in-law, and brother were laid to rest. I really hoped seeing their graves would help me with closure.

I was glad to be heading home with Shekinah. Lovemore

had supplemented the needed funds for the trip, but there was enough only for Shekinah and me. Simba would stay behind with his father. Shekinah was as good as gold during the 20-plus hours on the flight and the 6-hour layover along the way. As I predicted, everyone loved Shekinah when they saw her. I did go to the village and saw where they had buried my mother, as well as my brother and sister-in-law. It was kind of surreal but seeing their graves helped me to accept their deaths.

Three years had passed since I had last seen my country. While we were away studying in the United States, life had grown more difficult for most Zimbabweans. As in most places, it depended on where you lived. The lifestyle of those living in the more affluent suburbs did not seem affected, but I noticed that a number of businesses had closed in the cities or moved elsewhere as rampant inflation started to take a toll on the nation's economy.

Shekinah and I remained in Zimbabwe for the rest of the summer, and I was pleased to have some ministry opportunities. I was asked to speak at my home church at an evening service. When we got to the place where I was supposed to speak, a community center, nobody knew where to find the keys. As a result, I had to speak at an open air meeting, something I had never done before. Ironically, I had planned to speak on fear. So my own fear was put to the test that night. But what a joy when two men gave their lives to the Lord that night! Glory be to God.

A few days before we were scheduled to leave, Shekinah spiked a fever as well as showing symptoms of a cold; she seemed just miserable. The doctor diagnosed her with pneumonia and prescribed antibiotics. I did not look forward to traveling with a sick child, but we made it home safely. The trip had been a success. I had reconnected with friends and spent time with my family. They got to know Shekinah and we all chuckled at her fear of bugs.

Chapter 11
A Turn of Events

As we traveled back to the United States, I found I was looking forward to returning to my new home. Aside from Shekinah still recovering from pneumonia, it felt good to be getting ready for a new school year. My husband had met us at Newark Airport and, after spending a couple of days visiting Lovemore in New Jersey, drove our little car back to Rhode Island. Felix had developed a headache by the time we arrived in Barrington, but this was a common occurrence due to his erratic work schedule, with a lot of overnight shift hours. The following day was registration day and, with my husband having already graduated, it was just my turn to register for my third year of classes. I was quite excited. Shekinah was feeling better, and her father would care for her when I was in class; when I came home, he would go to work and I would watch our children.

After returning to campus from Zimbabwe where I had put closure on the deaths of my mother and my brother, and my

daughter was still recovering from pneumonia, I remember my neighbor asking, "What else can go wrong?" I had actually forgotten what she had said until she reminded me some time later.

Just before we went to sleep that night, my husband mentioned that his head was still hurting and he took two headache pills. We put our daughter into her crib, which was in the same room, and we went to sleep. Early in the morning around 6 am, my daughter woke me with her cries. I checked on her and she went back to sleep, but then something else disturbed me, my husband's breathing. I thought he was sleeping in an uncomfortable position, causing his breathing to be irregular, so I shook him a little and told him to sleep on his side so he could breathe well. That is when I saw that he was not responding. He was breathing but he was limp. He just lay there and when I tried to talk to him, I realized that he was unconscious. I screamed for my son to get the neighbors while I called 911. The first responders arrived almost immediately and I tried to explain what was happening.

Within a few minutes, our apartment building was surrounded by the sound of sirens and an entire rescue team: a fire truck, police cruisers and an ambulance. They rushed upstairs, and by then I was in a frenzy because I could not understand what was happening to Felix. An EMT checked his vital signs and, after a little deliberation, the police cruisers left. The firefighters stayed on to help carry my husband, a big man, down to the first floor. Once again, I felt that I was in a very bad dream and I would wake up soon.

Leaving my son with neighbors, I took my little girl in the ambulance with my husband. He was still unconscious when we arrived at the hospital, and I was numb. Felix remained in that state of unconsciousness for three days. Meanwhile, his doctors ran a battery of tests to try to diagnose what was wrong. Even at that early stage, they did caution me that they thought he was terminally ill.

On one of those days, as I was visiting Felix in the hospital, a social worker was waiting to talk to me with the doctor.

The news, from what they could tell, was that Felix had developed an inoperable mass in the brain and had six months at most left to live. That prognosis was impossible to process. I am not sure what the social worker said that day; I only recall that she asked a bunch of questions and made an appointment to come and see the children and me. She wanted to make sure the children were doing well and I was not planning to do something I might regret. She did help me to view things in perspective and to have a little hope. Life did not stop, but everything became totally altered for me. I was not sure whether I was coming or going. The college allowed me to register for three classes, and those classes gave me something to focus on amidst the chaos of uncertainty over Felix's (and our own) future.

A friend offered to watch Shekinah while I was in class, picking her up every morning and bringing her home in the early evenings during the week. She was the wife of Bishop Brown, pastor of the Church of God in Christ in South Providence. My son continued to take the bus to and from school and he tried to help me whenever he could. I still had no driver's license at this point. Sometimes I wonder how I survived those crazy and challenging days. Many of the college staff, as well as our fellow students, offered rides to the hospital. I had obtained a learner's permit just before leaving for Africa, but now wished I had pushed to get my license earlier on. However, thanks to the help of many friends, I did get to visit my husband and sometimes I took the children with me. It was hard to think about what was happening. I was still in a state of shock.

One thing stands out though; every morning and every night and sometimes during the day, a tune would play in my head. It's a melody I had never heard before and I found it comforting. Someone suggested that the Lord sang over me and others said that the Lord gave me a song in the night (Zephaniah 3: 17). I may never know, but the tune continued to play in my head all through this difficult time. I was reminded of a familiar poem "Footsteps in the Sand", in which the writer talks about walking

together with Jesus. During some of the lowest and saddest times of her life, however, she sees only one set of footprints and assumes the Lord had left her. But He assures her, "When you saw only one set of footprints, it was then that I carried you."

Gloria, my downstairs neighbor, showed up every morning around 5:00 am, usually bringing along her baby son, and she prayed with me. I don't recall what she prayed or even whether I participated, but Gloria's support meant so much to me. The College held weekly chapel services, where the other students surrounded me and prayed with me.

Sometimes I felt too overwhelmed to pray and I could only cry out to God, but the faculty, staff, and students participated in an all-night prayer vigil for my very sick husband. It was just so hard to believe that Felix had managed to drive us from New Jersey to Rhode Island just one night before he passed out and was taken to the hospital – and now he had a terminal illness with a timeline. What was going on?

Chapter 12
<u>The Longest Weekend of my Life</u>

My husband continued in the hospital for a month. Finally, when all of his vital signs were stable, he was sent home. A group of students rotated through helping us out and they also prayed with us. I'll never forget one particular youngster who was probably about 10 years old at the time; his parents were students at the college and he came over every afternoon. He read the Bible to my husband for an hour each day and then he would go home. He never accepted food or drink, but he was certainly one of the most polite and faithful young men I have ever met.

An added complication was that Simba had to get a cast for his knee due to a growth spurt that summer, so I now cared for a son in a cast, a baby daughter, and a very sick husband. Meanwhile, Felix's memory seemed to be getting more confused; he would go to the living room and couldn't find his way back into the bedroom. He was unable to care for our daughter as certainly as he was unable to care for himself. Despite the cast, however,

our son was a great help, whether it was watching his little sister, setting the table, or just being there.

Three or four weeks after his initial hospital stay, Felix awoke with a fever. I called Lorna, an American friend, who took his temperature, agreeing that it was dangerously high. An ambulance was called and he was taken back to the hospital. The doctor suspected an infection and started a course of antibiotics. I visited Felix every day except on those rare occasions when I was unable to find a ride to the hospital.

On one of those days when my husband was still in the hospital, my daughter suddenly started heading down the steep stairs from our second floor apartment, something she knew she was not supposed to do. I raced after her, but just as I got to the top stair, she missed a step and went tumbling down. She landed at the bottom of the stairs, and for just a second, she was silent. My heart missed a beat, and I feared she was dead. Was I going to lose another baby? Then came the ear-splitting scream. I picked her up and she was bleeding from the nose and mouth. My friend Pat, who had just arrived for a planned trip to the grocery store, drove us instead to the emergency center in Barrington. By then little Shekinah had stopped screaming, but her forehead looked so swollen, it scared me. The doctor examined her and ordered an x-ray. The x-ray technician suspected that my daughter had sustained no brain damage as, by that time, she was chattering non-stop, speaking words we could understand. Thankfully, the x-ray results indeed confirmed no brain damage.

Unfortunately, I could not share with my husband the trauma of Shekinah's fall nor my relief and gratitude at her recovery, and expect him to understand; he would now just stare vacantly. A good friend came to visit and, although Felix recognized us, he could no longer speak. I took the children to visit on Christmas day but my son became very uncomfortable in that room. Sadly, that was the last day my children saw their father alive.

On the 29th of December, a massive snowstorm blanketed Rhode Island, making driving treacherous. The previous day, my husband had been transferred to a nursing home across the bay from

us, but the roads had been cleared, and I was able to make it to the new location, accompanied by the children's social worker.   Felix's breathing was much labored even though he was helped by a respirator. I prayed with him and tried to encourage him, letting him know that everything would be okay, but he just stared at me, uncomprehending. By the following day, the governor was advising travelers to stay off the roads. The 30th was a Saturday, and indeed the weather did not look very inviting, so I decided to get out the iron and tackle the pile of laundry that my son had helped me wash.

The following day I planned to bring the children to see their father, following worship services at nearby Barrington Baptist Church where we had been attending. That night, however, I had a really unsettling dream; someone delivered to me a very small wooden container-like object. I was told that an old woman had died and I had gotten the best from her inheritance. This container was a small piece of furniture that served as a refrigerator and a stove at the same time. The top could be used as a stove and the front door opened to access a small freezer. I woke up soon after that and my spirit was restless. I could not focus on anything.

In the morning I felt too tired to go to church but my son decided to walk over by himself. When Shekinah finally woke up, I fed her and bathed her and got her ready for the nursing home visit. The dream was still nagging me, so around midmorning I called the nursing home to check on my husband's condition. They reported no change from two days ago, when I had last visited, and that news put my mind at rest. My son returned just before noon, and I prepared to give him a quick lunch prior to visiting Felix. Suddenly the phone rang and my heart skipped a beat. The voice on the other end was my husband's doctor, calling from the nursing home. He was telling me to sit down. He said that my husband had stopped breathing. "And did you resuscitate him?" I implored. He only said, "We did all we could, but your husband is gone." That is when I burst into loud, agonized cries. Simba asked me if it was his father. I nodded, and he stepped outside for a walk. I am sure he, too, needed to cry.

Chapter 13
Aftermath

Felix had been terminally ill; we knew his days were severely numbered and there was virtually no hope for his recovery. Still, I found I could not fathom the fact that he had left me. I cannot recall what I did next as the realization of his death tried to take root. I finally called the children's social worker, who advised me to try to rest, and that she would be over to make the needed calls to notify the family. As I awaited her arrival, I hugged my baby girl and wept. Simba returned just as Elizabeth showed up. Using my address book, this compassionate woman began calling members of my family and my husband's family in Zimbabwe. It was clear that her sad news triggered shocked reactions and tears. Felix's relatives indicated that they would gather the family together to make a decision regarding his remains and contact me. Initially they wanted to bury Felix in the United States and send a delegation from home to attend the funeral. They had second thoughts, however, deciding instead

to fly the body home, a decision that was amenable to me. In the end, however, the cost to fly my husband's remains to Zimbabwe forced a third alternative; the body would be cremated, and the children and I would be tasked with bringing the ashes back home to them.

While I was uncomfortable with that decision and dreaded the thought of my sad mission, I had to abide by the decision of my husband's family. In Zimbabwean culture, the marital relationship takes precedence as long as the spouse is still living, but if he dies, then his family takes charge. My husband's family, therefore, would give the orders as to what course to take. When my son learned of our orders, he was crushed and angry. Having left his home country four years earlier, he no longer felt connected and he certainly dreaded returning under these circumstances. Still, as a twelve-year-old, he had little choice, and the three of us would soon be making travel plans. As for me, I knew my husband was in heaven with the Lord. What was left was just a shell and not worth fighting over with my in-laws.

Elizabeth drove me to the nursing facility, encouraging me to take as much time as I needed to say goodbye. Felix lay there as though he were sleeping. I must have lingered in that room for an hour, believing my husband would wake up. As I prayed, I thought of the Bible stories I'd heard of people who had been restored to life. I waited for that miracle to happen to my husband, too. Finally I began to weep in agony, as the reality began to hit home. Felix was not going to rise from the dead.

I retrieved Felix's few belongings and left the nursing facility, a very distraught woman. I cried all the way back to campus. The college administration was making plans for a memorial service on campus and I barely remember what was being discussed. Meanwhile, Felix's relatives were also planning how we would return to Zimbabwe. I was in a daze and, if I made any contributions, I doubt they were helpful. I do recall that three couples generously offered to cover our airfare to Africa and back. When I mentioned this offer to my husband's family, however, they insist-

ed they would take care of everything, so I told the couples that I was grateful but had to wait for my marching orders from home.

My son had finally gone along with the plan to cremate his father's remains, deriving some comfort from knowing that I would take him to the funeral home where he would see his father one last time. When we arrived at the funeral home, however, the news was not good. My husband's body had just been removed for cremation, and Simba missed the opportunity to say goodbye to his father. We both felt devastated and betrayed, but we moved on to our next assignment, to prepare for Felix's memorial service, which would take place on campus.

An official from the funeral home delivered the ashes in a black plastic urn. It was the best they could offer since I could not afford a more presentable vessel. It did not matter. The fact was that my husband was gone. I found it hard to sleep that night. For a man as big as my late husband to have been reduced to a small box of ashes was very disturbing. I could not pray and I could not sleep. In fact, I slept very little until the day we left for Africa.

Meanwhile, the international student body told me they had collected some cash and wanted to do something for us as a family. During the time of Felix's hospitalization, these students had spent a lot of time with us, caring for us. They suggested buying a briefcase for carrying the urn, and that seemed like a good idea. That same night I discovered that the black plastic urn had a crack on one side, exposing the ashes, so these good friends set out to get that fixed as well.

Due to time constraints, the students opted to find a funeral home closer to the college, rather than making the trek back to the original funeral home near the nursing facility. The students shared my story with the funeral director, who was so touched by my circumstances that he offered to donate an urn. They returned with my husband's ashes in a beautifully finished wooden urn. Strangely, it looked like the gift I had dreamt of on the day my husband had died.

Many folks came to Felix's service, including Felix's close friend Lovemore from New Jersey, my friend Emma from Pennsylvania, and Pastor Terry King and his wife from Maryland; it was Pastor King who was ministering in Zimbabwe and had first recommended RIBI to us. When I saw them I could not contain my grief. The service itself seemed like a blur.

On the following day, the president of the college asked about my future plans. I explained that I would complete my education when I returned from Zimbabwe, and he prayed for us. Meanwhile, my husband's family had booked our airline tickets and instructed me as to where we should retrieve them. Emma and several other friends packed our clothes. While I was not very involved in the packing process, I made certain that I did not leave the urn behind. Since Shekinah would require most of my attention during the trip, Simba would be in charge of the briefcase with the urn. It was heartbreaking to think that my son would soon carry his father's remains from the USA to Africa.

We would fly out of Boston on January 11th. Now that we were about ready to board the plane, I was nervous about going home. I dreaded facing my family and my late husband's family all alone. I felt stripped of my covering. Since leaving Zimbabwe in 1996, Felix had been unable to return home. Now we were bringing him home in the form of ashes. Of course I knew it was not my fault, but I still felt responsible for not bringing my husband home alive. I think I know how Naomi felt (Ruth 1:20). Once again, it felt as though I were dreaming - and I would wake up at some point.

Chapter 14

Back to Africa: part 2

As the children slept in the plane, I tried to imagine my late daughter, my parents, and my husband all celebrating in heaven, but my thoughts could not remain there for long, because that place still felt too raw. After a six-hour layover in London, we began the final leg of our flight. As we neared the Harare Airport I began to feel anxious. I was careful not to betray any sign of anxiety as I did not want my son to worry. Because we had to wait to collect a stroller, we were among the last passengers to exit the plane. As soon as the plane landed (I later learned) all of my waiting family members, my husband's family and our friends who came to the airport started weeping. The wailing and weeping got worse when we finally entered the terminal. I just continued pushing my daughter in her stroller and my son carried his father's ashes in the briefcase.

As soon as I saw our families waiting in the airport, the room seemed to go black, I started to cry, and then briefly passed

out. Once we were outside I revived and was ushered into a car belonging to my husband's uncle. A police procession accompanied our cars to my mother-in-law's house. While it is not typical for police to escort a funeral, there were so many cars in our cortege that the police were brought in for safety and traffic control. We headed to my mother-in-law's home, which would be the site of the funeral, and since my former home was now being leased to another family, the children and I would also stay there. Everything seemed to happen so quickly. I kept wishing I could stop the clock and turn it back. The brook had gone dry and I couldn't fathom how I'd get through the next day, not to mention the rest of my life.

The details for the funeral service were arranged; on the day preceding the funeral, an endless procession of relatives queued through the house, and each one wanted to hear the account of how Felix had died. After a while, my response seemed mechanical, aside from the times I broke down and wept. Two days later, jet-lagged and weary and simply filled with grief, we held Felix's funeral and his ashes were buried.

The ride back from the graveside seemed to take forever. If only I could lie down and sleep and wake up to find that I had dreamt everything that had happened over the last few months! As a mother of a two-year-old, however, I had no choice but to pull myself together. At age twelve, at least my son seemed to be handling his grief. There were enough baby-sitters and caregivers that I knew Shekinah was in good hands. She would come to me if she wanted to eat or sleep, or if she had been frightened by an insect. Shekinah did not care for bugs at all; at least her little screams of fright created some levity during our sad time.

Unlike American funerals, which may last an hour, perhaps preceded by calling hours and followed by a graveside service, a funeral in Zimbabwe usually continues for several days. In addition to the service of burying the body or the ashes, the family of the deceased hosts' family members, close friends, and neighbors over a period of several days. The mourners are typically

wailing as they arrive at the house; once inside they give words of comfort to the bereaved, sing hymns and choruses, and care for one another. The female mourners remain inside the home, while the males camp outside. Most of the chairs are moved outside for the men; at night they build a bonfire, not just to keep warm but to "announce" to the community that they are in mourning. Others from the community see the fire and come over to offer comfort and support. Meanwhile, inside the house, the female guests sit on rugs, consoling the bereaved women of the family. Many guests spend several nights, being available to console at any time, day or night. In the mornings, someone is up early, boiling tea in a large container. It was not unusual for a visitor to hear the gospel during one of these funerals and come to faith in Jesus Christ.

During the funeral vigil, I remember waking up at night on several occasions; whenever I did, there was always someone by my side to listen and sympathize; I never felt alone. Meanwhile, Simba stayed with his cousins; his aunts made sure he was okay.

After the funeral, Simba, Shekinah, and I moved from my mother-in-law's house to my brother Benjamin's home, about 20 minutes away. My brother, his wife and their two children were actually renting space in a house where another family lived as well, so our quarters were a bit cramped. More people came to visit us there. Finally, the memorial service took place.

In Zimbabwe the memorial service takes place about one month after the burial. It differs from the funeral in that it is not considered a time to grieve but a time to remember the deceased and encourage his loved ones to carry on. The memorial service includes the testimonies of friends and lasts a full day.

The memorial service was held at my mother-in-law's house as well. I was encouraged to see so many dear friends. A children's choir from the school where I used to teach came with their director, Ms. Marimira, and they performed several beautiful songs. Following custom, family members and friends gave me scripture verses and words of wisdom to take me through life

as a widow. I could barely contain my tears when my brother Benjamin spoke; but he advised, "This is not a day for tears. It is a day we equip you to go on with life," so I tried to listen closely to all that was said. A couple of my former pastors were present. One of my husband's cousins gave me a word to take with me and it is found in Psalm 91. Friends from Scripture Union had very encouraging words for Simba and me. They played guitars and sang songs. One was Brother Asafa who had driven me home to visit my mother before I left for the USA the first time. These were surely different circumstances.

Another tradition is the distribution of the deceased's clothes and furnishings. Much as I argued with Simba's uncles, they insisted that my son take his father's clothes. I knew he would not wear them. Another tradition concerned remarrying into the family. One can choose to have someone else take the late man's wife as his own if she chooses the second man.

Among my list of possible suitors were Felix's uncles, cousins, and brothers. However, if I chose not to marry a relative, I was to request a bowl of water, and   symbolically wash my hands of this option, to signify my lack of interest in marrying any of these men. This option would also indicate a willingness in having the family check on the children periodically. This was a funny ceremony to me. All of the men looked polished and wishing to be picked including those with wives already. (Polygamy is legal in my country.) The surprising thing was that some wives were encouraging me to select their particular husband so we could be wives together in this new marriage. I had decided a long time ago that I did not wish to marry any of Felix's relatives. I therefore gave the water to the aunt, which appeared to infuriate a number of the men – but I just couldn't face a marriage of obligation to a man in whom I had no interest. Furthermore, I still needed to complete my education in the United States.

With the funeral and memorial service behind me, I was then called aside by Felix's relatives to discuss the airline tickets. I was dismayed to learn that our tickets from Boston to Harare

had been purchased with borrowed money; I was being asked to repay the cost before I could get our return tickets. I was shocked! Not only did I not have the funds but I had been given a false idea that the cost of tickets had been covered. Furthermore, I couldn't help remembering the three offers I had turned down - and I felt like the Lord had let me down, too. How would I come up with that much money? Thankfully, my brother Kudzai approached the relatives and intervened. They came to the agreement that they would use the rental money from my house and apply it to the cost of the tickets.

As I struggled with the crisis surrounding the cost of the airline tickets, I was being actively courted by one of my husband's cousins and his wife. They kept urging me to join forces and marry him. Their plan was that the cousin and I would earn the living while his wife would be responsible for childcare and housework. Still, I could not do it. Then the wife started arguing about how much education a woman needed, anyway. Eventually they gave up; I suspect they decided I was simply not worth their efforts.

I was finally given the tickets and we prepared to return home. I was happy – or maybe it was simply relief - to be flying back to the USA with my two children. I wondered where the Lord would lead us.

Chapter 15
I Just Need a Place to Lay my Head

As soon as we returned to campus, I was faced with a conundrum. One of the first people I met with was the president of the college. Surprisingly, he urged me to return to Africa, thinking it best that I be surrounded by family. Having just lost my husband, the thought of losing my opportunity to earn a college degree was unthinkable! The president then sent me to the college's financial advisor, who informed me that I had 30 days to find alternative housing. The problem was that, as a mom, I was ineligible to live in the "Girls Dorm", but as a newly single woman, I would also be barred from the "Married Couples" quarters.

Where would I find housing in 30 days? On the bright side, the next semester didn't start until September – and this was only March – so I had a few months before I had to think about classes. Simba had told a classmate, Nick Peck, of our plight and his mother stopped by to see if she could help. First, Leslie drove me to the Division of Motor Vehicles so I could test for my driver's

license. Additionally, she invited us to live with her family until we could find more permanent accommodations. She had a guest room where Shekinah and I could sleep, while Simba would share Nick's room. Finally, she helped me secure a part-time job at a daycare center which also had a space for Shekinah. Leslie was a gift from God, and one of those angels I will never forget.

In light of the housing problem, I really wondered whether I should continue at the same college. Leslie suggested we go together to talk to the president. I was reluctant but we did go. While he initially seemed offended that I had brought a friend, he insisted he still wanted me to continue as a student, despite the lack of housing for the children and me. "I understand what you are going through," he told me. What? While I had said little up to that point, I then suggested, "If ever you find yourself in a foreign country with two young children, after losing your spouse, please tell me you understand then, not right now – because you don't understand right now." My outburst got his attention, because he apologized and admitted he did not fully appreciate my dire situation. He asked what the college could do for me, other than housing.

So I made plans to continue with my classes, and the president arranged for help in getting me a work permit. Leslie and her husband Steve were so gracious to us, taking us in and welcoming us when we had no place to go. We stayed with them for five months, but as the end of the summer approached and they had family coming to visit, I felt it was time to say goodbye and find a more permanent place to live. I had considered homeless shelters, but they had separate men's and women's sections, which meant that Shekinah and I would be in one area, and Simba would be sheltered with men; while we were desperate, I did not like the idea of my teenaged son being housed in the men's dorm. Arline, my Native American "mom" had offered to house us temporarily – but she had room only for my daughter and me, which meant I still needed a place for my son. Pastor Jim Davis at Barrington Baptist Church had been so helpful to us in the past, and I asked

him and his wife Gail if they could possibly keep Simba. They were about to leave for vacation, but assured me they would pray about my request and contact me on the Sunday they returned.

We left Leslie's house on a Saturday evening and headed over to Arline's apartment. She had offered to house us for the night, then Pastor Jim would give me their decision about Simba in the morning. Arline, as a Native American, had informed me that she would be attending a Pow-Wow in Connecticut that day. If she were not home when we arrived at her house, it would just mean she was delayed in traffic. She was not yet home at 8:00 PM when we arrived, so we parked the car in the parking lot and my children and I waited. Around 9:30 I really needed to find some food for the children and I worried that "Nana", as we called Arline, might not make it home that night.

I drove the short distance across the border to Massachusetts, where I knew we would find some food and lodging. Although I was able to buy a meal for the children, I found all of the motels and inns in the area were fully booked. It was football season and we were "out of luck" as one hotel manager told us. We drove back to Nana's, but still she had not returned. Shekinah had fallen asleep and both Simba and I were feeling tired. I decided to stay in the parking lot and wait for Nana. I moved the car seat to the front, and my son climbed into the back seat and soon fell asleep. Sometime around midnight I heard sirens. Within a few minutes, my little car was surrounded by four police cruisers. What had I done?

"Get out of the car and put your hands where I can see them!" one officer admonished me and my son. Simba was groggy with sleep as we complied. The officer then looked at my driver's license and student ID, and noted that I was a student at the Bible College. What was I was doing in the parking lot at this late hour with my children, he wondered. I explained that we waiting for my friend. He claimed that someone in the apartment complex had called the police and reported a suspicious car in the parking lot. I insisted I was not there to cause trouble and just needed

to wait for my friend so we would have somewhere to sleep that night. But the officer protested that the parking lot was not safe for a mother and children and that I needed to find a hotel. I explained that the nearby hotels were fully booked and he advised me to try my luck in Providence.

The police cruisers were not about to leave until I started driving. Not eager to drive into a big city after midnight, I headed east toward Fall River, which is a straight route where I thought I might find lodging. Again, none had room for a mother and two children, so I turned around and headed west toward Providence. As a new driver, I had almost no experience navigating around the city. When I saw a sign for Cranston, I realized I must have missed an exit and driven right past Providence. I woke Simba up to help with directions and we finally found the Biltmore hotel in Providence. Once again, we got the response that it was fully booked. I was tired and discouraged. I decided to drive back to a local supermarket and park in their lot. Once I parked there, I beseeched the Lord, "Lord I am tired and am no longer a safe driver to be on the road and I have nowhere to go with the children. I am going to pull over between these cars which seem to be parked here permanently and I will go to sleep and I know you will protect us." Then I called Nana one more time. She finally got home and urged us to come to her apartment. We arrived at 3:00 AM and Nana prepared a place for us on the living room floor. But despite being exhausted mentally and physically I could not sleep. I just lay there until morning. I would soon hear the verdict on my request to pastor Jim and his wife Gail.

I got ready for church and left the children, still asleep on the floor, with Arline. After the service I sought out the pastor and his wife. They told me that they had prayed about my situation. "Since you are now Simba's only parent, we do not want to separate him from his family," they said. Right then I felt my heart sink. The next thing I would hear was that they could not take Simba. But that is not what I heard. "So we have decided to take all three of you. You can stay with us until you find a stable home."

What a provision! My daughter and I would share the basement room, and my son would share a room upstairs with the pastor's son who was of the same age. I was so grateful to the Lord for this couple!

We lived with the pastor and his family until we secured an apartment through the Coalition for the Homeless. I must say, you do not know a person until you live with him or her. Jim and Gail are the best examples of Christian love I have met in my life. They cared for us as if we were their kin. The pastor's house may have been small, but their love for us was monumental. We felt like we belonged.

When my family eventually moved to our new apartment, these dear friends helped us transport our few belongings and settle in. In addition, the Coalition which had located the apartment, also helped with furnishings and second-hand clothing, especially the kind of attire I would need as I neared graduation and looked ahead to starting a new career. What a great and un-expected blessing!

Chapter 16
Walking with Him, Day by Day

Not having to worry about a place to live was such a huge relief, and it gave our family a chance to grow and settle into a more normal routine. By this time, though, my studies and work schedule made it difficult to spend enough time with my children. Thankfully, Simba was a competent student, but he missed his father and often talked about him. I knew he was hurting inside. I was working part-time at the daycare center where Shekinah attended. Her days were long, however, often starting at 6:30 AM when I would drop her off and work a few hours. Then I would head to campus for classes, and return to the daycare center and put in a few more hours until closing at 6:30 PM. While I was thankful she had a safe place to go while I attended classes, I longed for the day when we both could spend more time at home.

One day I'll never forget was when the Lord provided funds for us. I remember that particular day because there was

no school, perhaps a teachers' in-service day, so my son was at home and the only food in the house was two cans of green beans and a box of pasta. In actual fact, there was nothing for breakfast, lunch nor dinner. I had a plan, though. I was going to meet with my friend Frieda, from Uganda. I had given her some African outfits to sell for me and I was hoping she had had some success.

After dropping off Shekinah at day care, I headed to campus but was late for class and ended up at the back of the lecture hall, where I was unable to get Frieda's attention. During class break, I maneuvered to the front of the room, but Frieda had already gone to the Fellowship Room, so I just found a seat in the front and waited. While I waited, a South Korean friend stopped by and asked about the children and me. I told her that they were doing well and so was I. She then handed me a yellow envelope. She had done this in the past, thrusting a $20 bill into my hands. I thanked her and said a thank you prayer to the Lord. I was grateful for this very thoughtful gift, although I lamented that it would not cover all that we needed.

Frieda did not return to class until the lesson was just about to start, so we did not get a chance to chat. With some money in my pocket, I decided to head home after class. I picked up some bread and milk and dropped it off for my son before returning to campus. During the few minutes I was at home, the phone rang. Pastor Jim told me that someone at church had left a check for us and asked when I could retrieve it. Needless to say, I headed right over to the church. Pastor Jim prayed for me and handed me an envelope. I opted to open it when I returned to campus.

To my complete surprise, I found a check for $500! As I shed tears of joy and relief, I yearned for an opportunity to tell someone what God had just done for me. On campus I headed to our class's prayer meeting. The class president stood up and related that the suit he was wearing was an unexpected gift from a friend. He added that he was changing the focus for that day's prayer time; instead of sharing our personal testimony as to how we came to Christ, he asked if anyone wanted to share a story

about some amazing thing God had done for him or her recently. Sure enough, I was the first one up, and testified how God had provided for us, crying tears of joy. Most of the students knew of my situation, and were very supportive; all were thrilled to hear of the Lord's provision for us.

Just before I sat down, my friend Frieda mouthed the words, "I have some money for you as well." I was stunned at how God works so fast, using so many different people and different avenues. My Korean friend did not know of our predicament; neither did the pastor who had given me the check, which turned out to be from an anonymous giver. The amazing ways of our great God!

Chapter 17

A College Graduate...Again

In 2003, the senior class started to prepare for our final year and graduation. I had mixed feelings about it all. The local Christian school had accepted me as a candidate for practical teacher training for the following year, so I was looking forward to that. Meanwhile, there were more student formalities as well as festivities to be celebrated. The baccalaureate service was an elaborate evening and my son walked me into the event. He looked all grown up and handsome. I was proud of him. I have always felt that I have been surrounded by angels in human form. Just before this event, some friends were heading to New York on a shopping trip; they decided to shop for me as well - and what a beautiful dress they brought me! I had had no interest in shopping for this or any of the other upcoming events, yet these ladies cared enough to see that I was well dressed and my hair was properly groomed. Because my husband would not be there, I had stopped caring. My friends' care and concern, however, became contagious, and I felt like a princess decked out in a beautiful crimson gown.

On the night of the baccalaureate, I felt composed and unemotional. The next event, however, was the commissioning service, held on the evening preceding graduation. That service was difficult; I was tearful, thinking of what might have been. On the one hand, I found myself missing my husband; on the other, I felt overwhelming relief thinking through all I had experienced to get to the point of graduation. By God's grace I was graduating - that in itself was a great accomplishment – and graduating with honors. Friends at Barrington Baptist Church had organized a graduation party for me. I felt like a huge weight had been lifted from my shoulders. I ached for my husband to be with us – but I knew he would have been happy for me – and today I was celebrating!

Although I had already taught school in Zimbabwe, I was still required to complete two semesters of practical training in the US to obtain a teaching license. This would take place after graduation. My training would take place at Barrington Christian Academy on the same campus as the church. I was able to place Shekinah at Wee Care, also on the same campus, for daycare. It was closer to home, which made the day a little shorter, and she seemed to be thriving better.

Our home through the Coalition for the Homeless had been the top floor of a three-family house. The Coalition allowed families to live in their home for two years, then encouraged each family to find a rental. The social worker responsible for our housing met with me at least once a week. Paula was a very kind lady who had just suffered through a divorce. We became close friends during the years in our Coalition home; Paula even attended my college graduation and celebration. I was in my junior year of college when we first moved in, so the agreement ended soon after I graduated. It would be hard to locate a new home on my part-time wages, but the Lord knew that – and I needed to stop feeling stressed about providing a home for my family. It was actually through the believers at Barrington Christian Academy that the Lord met our housing needs. Elsie, the Head of School, helped me find a temporary place and offered to cover the balance beyond what I could afford on my salary.

The Lord provided housing, and He also provided comfort. Shortly after we moved into our new home, my brother Kudzai Obadiah grew ill very suddenly. It seemed he had eaten something that was rapidly destroying his liver. Needless to say, I was very disturbed by the news. He told me he was very sick and his stomach was swollen. Within a few days, on the 23rd of October 2003, my brother went home to be with the Lord. I was devastated by the death of a much-loved brother.

Friends from BCA and Barrington Baptist rallied around us, comforting and encouraging us. But the healing wounds felt open again. The church offered grief share sessions, which helped me, work through some of the pain. I reread Jerry Sittser's A grace disguised: How the soul grows through grief. The head of my school gave me a CD with readings from Psalms, along with a book about the loss of an older brother or sister. God brought healing to my hurting heart, slowly but surely.

After my year of practical training at BCA, there was a burst of new enrollments and the school opened up another sixth grade class. I was offered this position and was able to enroll my daughter in the kindergarten there as well. Usually, Shekinah and I managed to get home by the time Simba was dropped off by the bus or by his football coach.

One of the things I realize as I look back is that I did not plan on what to do next. I just lived one day at a time, looking to the Lord for guidance, and tried not to worry about the following day. After about three months in our temporary home, I was informed that my name was finally at the top of the list for Section 8 housing and that made my day! Once I submitted the needed documents, we moved into our new home. It was close to school and work, and even though the neighborhood was sometimes noisy at night, I loved our new home! The church came alongside me again and helped us settle in this new place, providing many gifts and gift cards. We needed all kinds of furnishings, so that was a big help. Soon our lives settled into a routine and, for the first time in ages, I began to feel like everything was going to be normal again.

One day in the fall, I was surprised to find the East Providence police at my door. I immediately worried, thinking something had happened to my son. The two officers asked if they could come inside and advised me to sit down. Their next words were a complete shock. They told me they had visited the rental office, asking for two families they could bless for Thanksgiving. They wanted to help families who had paid their rent faithfully and did not squabble with neighbors. My name was one of two they had been given. Wow! So that year the police blessed us with a Thanksgiving basket and Christmas gifts as well!

Chapter 18
I Couldn't Ignore the Pain
In My Arm

Soon after we settled into our new home, an old friend from Kenya returned to the States to continue her education. Valentine needed a place to stay until she found a job and then she would look for a place of her own. I offered her a place to stay temporarily. Together we started praying for her needs. For several weeks we prayed with no answer - or so we thought.

One morning I woke up and my right arm was hurting as if I had carried a heavy bag for a long time. I assumed it was from the weight of the textbooks I carried back and forth. After a week of discomfort, the arm was still sore, so I tried rubbing in some of the sports medication my son used for sore muscles. The arm continued to throb painfully, and I could hardly sleep. I had developed a fever over the weekend, but did not make a connection between the pain in my arm and the fever.

By Sunday morning the pain was so severe I could not eat, and stayed home from church. When Valentine returned, she urged me to have the arm examined at the local urgent care clinic.

There was a bug making the rounds that spring, and the waiting room was packed. My daughter waited with me. During the first couple of hours, the pain kept escalating. By the third hour, I had to lay down on the waiting room floor. My arm had continued to swell, looking as though I'd been bitten by a poisonous snake. My name was finally called, and I was shown into an examining room, where I tried to explain to the doctor what was going on. I recall hearing him tell me he was going to call the hospital right away so a surgeon would be on hand when I arrived. I do not remember much else after that as my body was overcome by toxic shock and I passed out.

Three days later, I regained consciousness in the intensive care unit of Memorial Hospital of Rhode Island. My arm looked like a claw. The surgeon came in to see me, telling me I was lucky to be alive. He did not believe, however, that he could save my arm. I had developed a very serious bacterial infection deep within the arm. Had he needed to cut any closer to the bone, the limb would have to go. I was very weak and stayed in the ICU for two more days before being discharged to a regular room. I was given heavy doses of Vicodin and morphine, and food tasted horrible. I lived on protein shakes but was still running fevers. I had noticed a suspicious spot on my lower arm and I was sent back for more surgery that same day. The continuing fever was due to the infection having spread to the lower part of my arm. This second surgery was not as extensive but it was deep and extended my hospital stay. Still, I was grateful because I still had my arm. In time I began to use the fingers a little. I never learned the source of the infection.

I have never seen such an outpouring of love as I received from parents and students at BCA, where I was teaching. I received many cards and gifts. While they were showering me with love and care, the staff and parents were also preparing meals for Valentine and the children. I am a truly blessed widow. I stayed in the hospital for eight weeks and was then discharged to home care. A visiting nurse would change bandages and administer

medications. The day after I got home, however, I suffered a seizure and returned to the hospital.

That night as I sat in my hospital bed, two friends from church came to visit: Suzanne Treichler and Dave Westberg; we had a unique divine experience. While we were praying, I felt a presence in the room, and I knew the Lord was with us. When we finished praying, Suzanne asked if I, too, had felt His presence. The following day, I was discharged and I went home to continue recovering.

During my hospitalization, my son had been featured for the first time in the Providence Journal. He was on the East Providence High School track team, and was setting new records in high, long and triple jumping; he also ran on the relay team which was also having a successful season. I read the first article while I was in my hospital bed and it brought me such joy amidst the trials of my infection. I have always been proud of him, but it was a huge blessing for him to excel in his efforts for the track team. A few weeks after I was released from the hospital, I started to drive again. As my pain began to lessen, I was weaned off the very strong medication and began to taste food again. Valentine found a job and was then able to afford her own home, so she left us, but I don't know what I would have done without her help with my children during my long hospital stay. I have scars on my arm but I also have a testimony from that dry brook.

Chapter 19
Moving

A fter several long months of recovery, I finally returned to my classroom shortly before the end of the school year. I will never forget my first day back. The head of school gave me time to visit all of the classrooms. The little kindergartners brought tears to my eyes as they told me how they had prayed for me daily. All of the teachers and students welcomed me so warmly. My own students presented me with a precious memory book filled with expressions of love and caring by students, parents, fellow teachers and church members. I could almost touch the love I felt from everyone and I thank God for each one. I was so grateful to be the recipient of such love and kindness and compassion.

While I was recovering, I heard stories of difficulties at the church, which shared a campus with the school where I taught. We had been attending this church and noticed there had been some attrition. Eventually, one of the pastors (not Jim) ended up leaving. Just before the school year was over, I felt the need to

pray. I had a free period, and found an empty classroom. Within a few minutes someone came looking for me and I was off for a drive with the head of school. The day was cloudy and kind of dreary. The head of school looked at me and started crying. She was sorry to report that there was a drop in student enrollment, which would in turn dictate a drop in staff; unfortunately, school policy mandated that the last person to be hired be the first to be let go. She wished things were different. This meant I would be bidding my students farewell at the end of that school year. She felt sure the Lord would take care of my little family and me as He had done in the past. But I felt like I was in another nightmare and I could not wake myself up. One thing I had struggled through with each loss was that, although I never once doubted that there is a God in heaven, I wondered whether He cared about what happened to me. How could God care about us when I was going to lose the job I needed to support my family?

Two friends, Joan Kirk and Suzanne Treichler, suggested we pray about the next steps, and how the Lord might use my skills and experience. As we prayed in Joan's house, I began to feel the assurance that God cared for me and His children cared for me, too. Yes, the proverbial ship was battered but the anchor was still holding. We came up with a plan; I would visit an inner-city pastor who had offered me a position in the past. I had not accepted the position because the church could pay very little. The new plan, if the pastor was still amenable, was for me to work at the church as a missionary and then these wonderful ladies would help me raise support as needed. This plan complied with my visa requirements, so I approached Bishop Brown and he agreed to hire me as Director of Christian Education at the Church of God in Christ in Providence. My duties included Sunday school teaching (both children and adults) and teacher recruitment, visitation of the sick and shut in, administration, even (occasionally) preaching. The church was able to provide a stipend and, as it turned out, the stipend and the support from friends was always sufficient to meet our needs. I thanked God for His provision and

for the ladies who prayed with me. I am eternally grateful to the Lord for the financial and emotional support I got from the people He sent my way.

Yet, although I was thankful to be employed, I did not feel I was doing anything consistent with my calling or training, so I decided to put my resume on a couple of job recruiting web sites. The first response I received was from a school starting up in Texas. The school had 75 families enrolled and needed an administrator. I knew I was no administrator so did not pursue that position. The next response came from a school in Williamsburg, Virginia seeking a middle school teacher, and I arranged with the head of this school for a phone interview. It turned out to be a very lengthy process, mainly because a storm was raging in Virginia, causing the connection to be severed time and again. We finally completed the interview, with the promise that the head of school would be in touch with me. I continued to hear from more schools, including one in Hawaii that made an offer, but I did not sense it was the right place for me. Eventually, I heard back from the Williamsburg School, this time from board member Lesley Hamer, also a co-founder of the school, asking if I could fit in another interview. I was ecstatic to hear from them and agreed to interview that same week, assuming it to be another phone interview. As it turned out, they were requesting an in-person interview! I would fly to Virginia, and the school would cover my expenses. Simba was old enough to take care of himself and Joan was able to watch Shekinah while I was out of town. Once again, weather intervened, and my flight was delayed in Philadelphia. I had never before set foot in Philadelphia, but Lesley made arrangements for me to spend the night at an airport hotel.

The weather cleared enough that I could fly to Williamsburg the following day. At the airport, I found Lesley holding a poster with my name on it. She drove me to my hotel while providing a rundown on the Williamsburg area. I was already impressed. The area was full of deer and other wildlife, gardens, parks, and a more rural landscape than our home in Rhode Is-

land. I found myself hoping this would be the place for me.

The interview would take place that evening after dinner. The school was located just behind my hotel, and the interviewing team consisted of Lesley and the head of school. I was relaxed throughout the whole process, and was told the board would be in touch. It seemed like ages before I heard from the school board and I fretted that they had found a more qualified candidate.

One morning in June, not long after the interview, I woke up very early and could not get back to sleep. I got up and took a walk along the beach near where we lived. It was before dawn and the children were still sleeping. Something was wrong and I could not concentrate on praying. After a short time, I headed back home and took a shower. As soon as I turned off the water, I heard the phone ring. My oldest brother had been diagnosed with liver cancer and I had been praying for him. My nephew Charles was calling. His uncle, my brother Jacob, had died. I struggled with losing yet another beloved family member.

Later that day, a group of ladies from the Kenyan Fellowship came over and prayed with me. Once again, I yearned to be with my family to grieve with them and share our loss but, once again, I was unable to go home for a sibling's funeral. Neither Shekinah nor I could sleep that night; my daughter ended up reading to me. We got through ten chapters before we both fell asleep!

It was in the midst of this sorrow that I got the good news that I had been hired by the school in Virginia. I was offered a middle school position at Providence Classical School in Williamsburg; when would I be able to return to Virginia? God's care and His timing were perfect. Simba had just graduated from high school, and he opted to remain in Rhode Island and attend college there, staying with friends who had offered him a place to live.

Rhode Island had been my home for nearly ten years. This move would be a big change for me, for all of us. I had developed many close relationships over the years of college and career, loss and provision. The Church of God in Christ, where I served as Christian Education director, held a farewell party and I had an

opportunity to say goodbye to many old friends and really process the reality that we were moving nearly 600 miles away from this place where we had experienced both great grief and great joy.

I knew God had blessed us with a new friend in Lesley. She located a rental for us in Williamsburg, only a short ride to the school. While we waited for our new apartment to be available, I stayed with the family of Erin, a school board member. Erin asked about my experience of emigrating from Zimbabwe and thought it worth sharing. She arranged an interview with a local newspaper, and the editor agreed to print my story. The article focused on how I had managed to survive the war for independence in Zimbabwe and then made my way to the USA. The writer portrayed me as a heroic figure. I was pleased that people were interested in Zimbabwe, but wished the article had given God – not me – the credit for all he had done to bring me this far. The experience did get me wondering about whether I might someday write my own story.

Early in the academic year, a new head of school was hired. She was delightful to work with, and I appreciated her interest in getting to know each of the teachers and students individually, and her concern for each one of us. When someone broke into my car, for example, it was Susan Oweis who drove me to the police station to report the incident. We discovered that the paperwork to retain my visa (required to be filed by employers for their employees) had not yet been submitted, so Mrs. Oweis saw that the materials were filled out and submitted for processing. I was thankful for this very supportive leader, who loved the Lord and was dedicated to her staff.

I was teaching a combined class of Grades 6 and 7. They were very polite, motivated students and it was not hard to love them. Many would leave appreciative notes for me on my desk. Three were recent adoptees from Ukraine (all in different families) and initially all three could speak only their native tongue; over the course of the school year, however, it was rewarding to see them develop their English skills to the point of complete flu-

ency by the end of the year. The students were intrigued by my own accent and background. As we discussed issues in our Bible class, I shared some of my life experiences and how God had provided for me or kept me safe. Hearing my story, the students suggested I write a memoir.

Chapter 20
The Brook is Dry

The following year I again taught a combined sixth and seventh grade class, with one eighth-grader in the mix. The students continued to encourage me to write about my life and I suppressed a smile when they suggested I dedicate the book to them. I had actually started writing but was struggling with the emotional toll it was taking. However, I assured the students I would do my best to complete my story.

In early March, the head of school summoned me to her office. My heart began to beat fast as I sensed something was wrong. Mrs Oweis informed me that my visa application had been turned down and that the school therefore had no choice but to terminate my services immediately. I could not believe my ears. I had awoken at dawn that morning, praying for everyone I could think of – but this was the last thing I could have imagined! Just when my world seemed to have attained some stability, it came crashing down again. Another brook had dried up.

Doreen, a fellow teacher as well as a parent, happened to be in the office and comforted me, but I could not stop crying. Although I was never given a reason for the rejection, I assumed that some of the contributing factors were the lateness of my application and the difficulty of non-residents moving from state to state after 9/11. The bottom line was that my US visa would no longer be valid after August 1st of that year. Originally, I had thought the decision could be appealed. Sister Margaret, a Roman Catholic nun who was also a good friend, had given me the name of an immigration lawyer whom she thought could help. The lawyer was kind enough to offer her services for free, although I had to pay a filing fee of over two thousand dollars to make an appeal to the US Supreme Court. As it turned out, the decision could not be appealed. Lesley suggested we consult with another immigration lawyer. We ended up speaking with three additional lawyers, but all concurred that I should leave the country before the date stated on my letter, just 3 months from the day I received the letter. That way, I could reapply for a new visa after one year. Alternatively, I could try to remain in the US after my visa expired and hope for clemency, but in the likely case I would not be allowed to remain, and found in non-compliance with the law, I would have to wait ten years to reapply. The question now was where would I go and how and when.

I was the guest of honor at yet another farewell party. The students asked where I was going and whether I would return to Williamsburg. I answered as truthfully as I could. They gave me some thoughtful gifts, including a keepsake book of memories, pictures, words of encouragement, and prayers from parents and teachers. Mrs. Oweis said something to the effect that she knew she would see me again. While she was kind to encourage me, it didn't seem very likely at that point.

Lesley suggested we consider some options that were open to me. One was an administrative position with Global Outreach Mission in Canada. I applied for and was offered this position, starting immediately. While a move to Canada had never been on

my radar screen, I was greatly relieved, and we proceeded to make the necessary arrangements with a Canadian immigration lawyer; Lesley's husband Jim helped me cover the considerable cost. The lawyer advised me about documents to present to border officials, along with my employment offer. The vice president of Global Outreach Mission (or GO Mission) would meet us there. Lesley then drove Shekinah and me to the USA/Canada entry point, a drive of over ten hours.

Prior to entering Canada, we met with GO Mission administrators at their US office in Buffalo, New York. I learned more about the mission and the position over dinner with the president, vice president, and secretary of this organization; their enthusiasm was an encouragement to me. The next morning we arrived early at the border, but found a long line of people already waiting. When my turn came, the receptionist at first declined to meet with me. Since my American visa was about to expire, she insisted there was no point in meeting with the counselors. After being persuaded by Lesley, however, she finally agreed to let me confer with a counselor.

Only the applicant was allowed inside the counselor's office. My counselor asked if I was in touch with my family back in Zimbabwe. I assured her that I was. While my parents and three of my brothers had died, I was still in regular contact with my remaining siblings. But the counselor did not feel my ties with my home country were strong enough. She asked, for example, to see the title deed to the house I still owned in Africa. Needless to say, I had not brought the document with me as it never occurred to me that it would be needed here or in the United States. Her concern was that, should I lose my job in Canada, I would become a burden to the government, as it seemed I was unlikely to return to my home country. It was true that I was hoping not to return to Zimbabwe, but not because of a lack of connection to my family. The problem lay in finding employment in Zimbabwe. There were few jobs, and for those jobs that did exist, there was no money to pay salaries. At that point, the Zimbabwe dollar had become

so hyper inflated that it was no longer in use. (Even the touted Z$100 trillion banknote had no value except as an object of curiosity.) Instead, international currencies including well-worn and filthy US dollars, euros, and South African rands had become the standard currency in Zimbabwe. With two children to support, a return to my home country was simply a risk I could not take. Conversely, the Canadian government, or at least its representative at the Buffalo entry point, felt I was a risk her country could not take. The vice president of Global Outreach Mission tried to explain that his organization would take full responsibility for me but his appeal fell on deaf ears. My application for a visa to work as a missionary in Canada was therefore rejected. One thing I was sure of, however, was that I was covered in prayer. Robin and three other parents had come to my house and prayed before we left for Buffalo. I knew they were continuing to pray, so whatever the outcome, the Lord was in it.

In light of this outcome, the vice president of G.O.M then asked if I would consider other fields where his mission has workers. Unfortunately, there were none in Zimbabwe, which would have been a logical choice. One of the few English-speaking African countries where G.O.M. did have an office was Sierra Leone. That seemed the best avenue open to me – if not exactly on my radar screen - and meetings were set up immediately to coordinate that. I was able to obtain a visa within one day. A job in Sierra Leone was better than no job. No one in Williamsburg was expecting us to return, least of all with news about Sierra Leone, but that's the news we had.

Chapter 21
Back to Africa: part 3

Before we left our home in Williamsburg in the summer of 2008, I still needed to pay the last month's rent. Since I was no longer receiving a paycheck, I had no means of covering it. One Sunday before the rent was due, I was at church, feeling burdened, but not wanting to share the need with anyone. Still overwhelmed at the prospect of relocating to Sierra Leone, I was not eager to stay around and socialize, so I headed to my car with Shekinah as soon as the worship service was over. Just as I was driving out of my parking space, however, the pastor approached me. Someone had left a money order in the offering plate and it was addressed to me. He handed me the envelope, indicating he did not know the identity of the donor.

I checked the amount when I got home; it was exactly $1000! The Lord was so good to me! To this day I do not know who blessed us with that money order, but just knowing that the Lord knows is enough. I pray the Lord will bless this individual as

only He can. At the end of our lease period, Shekinah and I moved in with our friends, Jim and Lesley, who opened their home to us. Simba came all the way from Rhode Island to bid us farewell.

I felt so unprepared for this new venture! Shekinah and I had secured our airline tickets and I was given a used laptop by the family of a former student. My friend Jean helped me set up a blog to communicate to friends back in Williamsburg what was happening and, most importantly, how they could pray for us. But, aside from occasional news reports about the recent horrendous civil war, I still knew precious little about Sierra Leone! G.O.M. felt that my teaching experience coupled with my Bible training and African upbringing made me an excellent candidate for the job, but I wished I could have had time to raise financial support and enlist more prayer partners. These are crucial preparations that can takes months, but due to my very short time frame, these preparations were left undone.

Meanwhile, there were more goodbyes to be said to our Williamsburg friends. Our friend Suzanne organized both a farewell party and a pool/birthday party for Shekinah. I was thankful to God for all these dear sisters and brothers in Virginia who came to wish us well; I would miss them dearly. Lesley and Jean accompanied us to the airport. Lesley assured us that we would return. She would do all she could do to help. I appreciated her optimism, and wished I could share her enthusiasm. Inside, I felt once again that my world was reeling out of control and just wished I could slow things down.

An unpleasant surprise awaited us at the airport in New York. My immigration lawyer had advised me that I would have to surrender my US visa (expiring that month) upon departure. When I tried to check my baggage, the airline agent informed me that my suitcases exceeded the weight limit, so I had to quickly determine which items to remove. I was also told to redistribute the weight of the other pieces. After repacking most of my belongings, I was then told I could not board the plane. Technically, I could board the plane, the problem was that, as I had no UK

visa, I would not be allowed to deplane in London, where I needed to change to a different airline. Even if I agreed to stay within the confines of an office in the airport, they still refused to let me board. The agent explained their reasoning, and I could see his point, but the problem for me was that I had to leave the USA within forty-eight hours to avoid violating INS regulations. What was I to do?

Lesley approached an agent from a French airline, but they could do nothing for us, either. We headed back to Lesley's house to spend another night. Finally, she contacted Royal Air Morocco and they were willing to book us on a flight through JFK. So, the following day, we headed to New York, then to Morocco for the first leg of our flight – and it was a long one. After our 4:00 AM arrival, we spent a long day trudging around the airport in Morocco, hoping to find someone who spoke English. We ran into many passengers who spoke Arabic, or French - and we managed to communicate with signs and a few words – but it wasn't until much later in the day that we met a young man who spoke English with a French accent. Like us, he was heading to Sierra Leone. In his case, he was going there for his own wedding; and he invited both of us to attend. While it was unlikely we could attend, we appreciated his kindness and thanked the Lord for sending this man to help in our time of need.

Arriving exhausted at Lungi Airport at 4:30 am, we were met by a Bible school student who was assigned to be our chaperone. We would stay at his father's house in Freetown, which was across the bay from the airport. Solomon engaged a taxi, and Shekinah and I climbed in. Within minutes both of us fell asleep. Before long a strong smell of fish wafted through the taxi and I woke up. I opened my eyes and looked around; groups of women appeared to be heading to market, carrying fish. In the months to come, I would often see these fisherwomen. They would angle by night, then board the ferry to Freetown and sell their fish, some fresh, some dried, at the market. Since the ferry ran throughout the day, they simply boarded the ferry for home when their

fish were gone. Shekinah and I now boarded the ferry for the first time, and the ride across the bay took about an hour. My daughter, however, was so tired she was able to sleep all through the smell of fish and the one-hour ferry ride.

The taxi disembarked in an urban area that had seen better days. Many buildings were dilapidated or lacked roofs. Clothing dangled off many walls. Makeshift shops were set up in front of homes. Taxis, motorcycles, and bicycles vied for space on the streets. Many young people seemed to be hanging about, with nothing to do. You could see the scars left by Sierra Leone's recent civil war and the signs of a resilient people who were just beginning to rebuild after so much death and destruction.

Sierra Leone had won independence from the UK only in 1961. Thirty years later, however, the young nation was rife with corruption, the economy had collapsed, and it had became one of the world's poorest countries, despite the presence of rich natural resources, including diamonds. As a result, civil war erupted, ostensibly between the rebel Revolutionary United Front and the Sierra Leone Army, and only coming to an end in 2002, thanks to intervention by the United Nations and the British government. By then thousands of civilians had been killed and millions displaced, but some of the most heart-wrenching experiences were those suffered by children who became victims of the war. Some were conscripted as soldiers[1] while other children were victims of rape and/or mutilation[2]. This was the land that would be our new home. I hoped and prayed I could serve these broken people in a broken land.

When we arrived at Solomon's father's house, we discovered there was no running water; electricity was available at most

[1] *see, for example, Ismael Beah's memoir A Long Way Gone, which details his appalling experiences as a child soldier*

[2] *see, for example, Mariatu Kamara's The Bite of the Mango for her shocking account of losing both hands through the actions of rebel soldiers*

two days a week. We soon became objects of curiosity, attracting frequent visitors who wanted to look at the American tenants. The house tended to be noisy, not only with street noises but with chickens clucking through the rooms. The lack of privacy proved challenging but what was most concerning was that my usually bubbly and happy daughter had become so sad. After a couple of weeks, I contacted G.O.M. to inquire whether we might look into other affordable accommodations. Our next temporary home was a lodge, and it was a big improvement. The water was clean and drinkable; we had a generator to provide electricity during blackouts, and we even had some measure of privacy despite living with others. Solomon continued to help us, warning us not to speak up in public places lest we be taken advantage of as foreigners. Sierra Leoneans have great skill for negotiating and Solomon was no exception; one day we waited nearly an hour while this young man negotiated the price of some bananas.

My first two challenges were finding a more permanent place to live and finding a school for my daughter. Despite the dismal economy, it was still very difficult to find a decent, affordable home. One problem was that renters were required to pay an entire year's rent in advance. For us, that meant coming up with at least $10,000 in US dollars for a home in a middle class area. Our choices ranged from renting a room to renting an entire house in a preferred location like Juba Hill, where there is electricity all the time, in which case the up-front amount would double. At this point, I was not yet receiving a regular income from G.O.M.

The other issue had to do with my daughter's schooling. We visited the North American International School in Freetown; I liked this school as it was set up like a school in the states, with the kinds of curriculum and programs with which Shekinah would have been familiar, but the yearly tuition was $9,000. The head of school was very welcoming and we discussed various tuition payment plans, should I opt to send my daughter there. I thought it might be manageable if I could find a reasonable place to rent.

Meanwhile I got word that my support was not coming in as quickly as I would have liked, but G.O.M officials were not overly concerned. About this time, we met a missionary couple, Jackie and Larry Owens, church planters who were staying at the same lodge; they were also from Virginia, although they had been based in Zambia for the past four years. They had been looking for a house to rent, and were about to sign a lease for the next two years. (Multiple-year leases resulted in a discounted rental rate.) This couple kindly offered us a space in their new rental. They were anticipating the arrival of a colleague, but it would not be for a while, and we could use her space in the meantime. I contacted my mission about this plan and they worked out a temporary arrangement with Larry and Jackie while we thought and prayed things through. We would contribute toward the meals and the rental cost. The house was spacious, had a generator, and the couple welcomed us with open arms. It was good to have a home in a real house, but by this time I had started to have misgivings about my calling to Sierra Leone, and had to pray seriously about why I was there.

The Owenses had hired a young Leonean, Stephen, to oversee their garden. Shortly after we moved into the new house, Stephen's young son developed a fever. He was just over a year old. He seemed to be recovering, but then got worse and within a week, he died. We were all devastated because we had fallen in love with this sweet little boy. Due to the lack of mortuary space, he was buried the same day he died. What broke my heart was that his mother never got to kiss her little boy goodbye before he was buried. Friends had come to visit and mourn from surrounding areas, sharing their own stories of grief with this young mother, but I understood only too well the pain in her face. I needed to talk with her about my own loss, and how the Lord had sustained me. She listened and we prayed together and I could see that it comforted her to talk with someone who knew from experience what she was going through.

While they awaited the arrival of a large container of materials, Larry and Jackie had started a children's outreach as a precursor to setting up a Sunday school program. Many children participated and were thrilled to learn that, if they answered questions correctly, they received a Bible. Books of any type were hard to find in Sierra Leone. Soon parents started coming for Bibles as well. We quickly realized that many of the adults, especially women, could not read. Their education had been disrupted by the war, so the Owenses and I tried to meet this need by setting up an adult literacy class. Because many of the mothers spent their days at the market, we held our class in the early evenings.

While I worked at developing a curriculum for the adult literacy class, I was growing more concerned about my own daughter's education and our future as a whole. There were neither bookstores nor libraries in Freetown, but I was able to find a few books to use in home schooling my daughter.

I started visiting some of the eighteen schools Global Outreach operated in Sierra Leone. My job was to evaluate the progress and administration of the schools, and recommend changes, if warranted. Most of the schools were housed in sound buildings, and the students seemed to be learning, but I did note a few issues. I was especially disturbed by one school, for example, where some students had no chairs. Their parents were paying tuition but it had been siphoned off for something other than their kids' education. In this case I was able to locate and fax the appropriate documentation to correct the misuse of funds. In any case, these schools were an improvement over the schools run by the government. We saw one such school that met in a former chicken coop; over 900 students had been crowded into this very inadequate space.

I had been continuing to have reservations about our life in Sierra Leone and felt it was time to make a decision about our future here. My daughter needed to be in school and we needed a stable place to live. I conferred with my contacts at G.O.M., who were very understanding. I brought this need before the Lord,

and enlisted the prayers of our supporters and friends.   I heard of an opening at the North American International School in Pretoria, South Africa. My husband's brother and his family lived in Pretoria, and I suspected it would be a much healthier place for my daughter. I wondered if that might be an option. I called my brother-in-law and asked if we might stay with them for a while.

Chapter 22

Waiting on the Lord

My brother-in-law and nephew met us at the airport in Pretoria on that October day in 2008. I had not seen Kuda since he was a little boy, about fifteen years earlier. I felt relieved even just to be in the airport. South Africa was a modern country that offered the infrastructure and conveniences that were lacking in war-torn Sierra Leone. Shekinah's whole outlook changed and I was relieved to see her smile and bubbly personality again. If we were to stay in South Africa, we knew that we would have to travel to Zimbabwe periodically to get new visas (South African visas were good for 90 days) but this was a country that let us hope.

When we arrived at the house that would be our home for over a year, we found that it was actually only a small two-bedroom apartment. Shekinah and I would occupy my nephews' bedroom and they would be relocated to a small balcony-like room. I was touched by this gesture and really appreciated their sacrifice.

Another relative had come to look for work in South Africa, and he would be living in the apartment as well. Due to the dire economic situation in my home country, many Zimbabweans were flooding into South Africa to find work. Runaway inflation left the Zimbabwe dollar nearly worthless; one of the paper currency denominations was actually the $1,000,000 bill! At one point, eight of us lived in that small apartment in Pretoria, although there had been as many as twelve, when other male relatives came to look for work. Although it was a tight squeeze, sharing living space and one bathroom, everyone made the best of it and we were always treated as beloved family members.

My position at the North American International School of Pretoria was temporary and lasted only through the end of the school year. I volunteered my services at the church we attended and was asked to assist with their Sunday school program. Even though I was not paid, it felt good to be doing the Lord's work again. Friends in Rhode Island provided financial support making it possible for us to contribute to the needs of all of us. Friends from both Rhode Island and Virginia sent care packages and other gifts. Shekinah and I were fortunate to be living with family in South Africa. Indeed our living situation was cramped, but we had experienced the shortages and devastation of Sierra Leone and now felt incredibly blessed. I had very little hope of returning to USA. I thought that boat had long sailed and it would take the hand of God for me to get back here – and it did.

In the meantime, I learned that, even in comparatively modern and thriving South Africa, life can be hard. I had an opportunity to work at a day care center near our home. The director was looking for a substitute caregiver with teaching experience and I was asked to assist in a class of twenty-plus three-year-olds. There was no lesson plan so we had to improvise and this turned out to be a real learning experience for me. Two things struck me. One was the poor nutrition offered to these little ones. The children were given black tea and a very small sandwich, so meager compared to the Head Start meals or school lunches parceled out

to children from low-income families in the US. The other thing was the lack of stimulating toys and activities, coupled with corporal punishment. At naptime the children had trouble settling down and going to sleep, perhaps partly due to hunger. While I was inclined to read a storybook or play music to soothe the children to sleep, one of the other teachers held up her shoe and warned them that she'd give a boot to any child whose eyes were open. I was appalled at the idea of threatening three-year-olds, but was told it was the only thing that worked. The kids seemed terrified and all kept their eyes closed. If any of them stirred before naptime was over, they were told to shut their eyes and go back to sleep. I vowed that I would never again work at a place like that unless I was given authority to make decisions that could positively impact the lives of these young children.

Early in the summer of 2010, I was surprised to receive an email message from Lesley back in Williamsburg. She wanted to let me know that a local church was looking for a Christian Education Director. Not only had I worked in Christian education, but I was also a former member of that church, and they were willing to apply for a visa for me. Was I interested? I could hardly believe it. Would I actually be able to return to the United States? To see my son again? This news was a truly unexpected answer to my prayers!

Epilogue

As I write this, several years after returning to my adopted country, I am happy to report that I am now a Green Card holder and I hope to one day be a US citizen. But more importantly, I am thankful to be a citizen of Heaven, to be a child of the Heavenly Father who knows what we need even before we ask. When Elijah's brook ran dry, God sent him to a widow. He had special plans both for Elijah and for the widow. I certainly never anticipated living in so many different homes, many of them no more than a room, in so many different countries. My son Simba is now a father to a three year old girl and twins, a boy and girl who are 18 months old. My daughter Shekinah is a sophomore at a College in Virginia. Whatever else is in my future, I am thankful to have a loving God to walk through it with me. No matter how dark or long the tunnel, there is light at the end of the tunnel because "with God all things are possible". (Luke 1:37)

Acknowledgements

A special thank you to Caleb Monfreda, Megan Lorincz, Taylor Henry Dahmen, Joshua Sparks, Christopher Cordasco, Isobel Bishop, Libby Doucette, Destiny Pacella, Elizabeth Henry, Alexander Svinicki, Irina Richards, Sophie Quiram, and David Frye, for encouraging me to write this book. You are wonderful friends and you were a great class. Without you, this story would not have been written.

Thanks to my friends and family from Barrington Baptist Church, the ones who have been there and continue to be there for me and my family. You have been a source of comfort, pulling us through the tough times and making us know how blessed we are to have you in our lives.

Allison Lake Brown, thank you for the dried brook painting. It's a beautiful masterpiece.

Thank you to pastor Jim Davis and his wife Gail, and Steve and Leslie Peck for your ability to love this African family.

A special thanks to Dave & Carol Westberg and to Jim and Lesley Hamer, all your perseverance does not go unnoticed.

I am immensely grateful to the wonderful group of friends who organized groups of people for me to share my story because they thought it was worth sharing: Mary-Ruth Franklin, and Barbara St. Pierre. I would also like to thank Sue Gablinske for organizing a women's conference so I could share my story. Thank you all for your encouragement.

Thank you to my friends who have stood by us during our times of deep sorrow, BBC Family, Jabez and Gloria Rapaka, Malcolm & Joan Kirk, Ray & Donna Uritescu, Dave & Terri Lorincz, Mike & Robin Doucette, Jean Henry and Harriet Machie.

I am grateful to the following friends who read and corrected my very raw manuscript. Your input was very helpful: June Bodden, Susan Franz, Suzanne, Judy Bono and Barbara St. Pierre. I thank you for helping me create a book that people can actually read. My deepest thanks to Ann Bell, an exceptionally gifted writer and author who read and reread my manuscript, offering me invaluable comments and endless support.

Special appreciation to Susan Oweis who wrote the forward to my memoir. You serve graciously and beautifully. You deserve far more applause than you receive. Thank you!

A very special thanks to my amazing editor Nancy E. Christy who is such a blessing. She knew what to edit and what not to edit. She checked the historical facts for me to make sure I had everything correct. You are a very patient and faithful friend and I cannot thank you enough for all you did including setting up the website for me. I am truly grateful to you.

A special thanks to Dr. Towera N. Loper for pointing me to Nyree and for being a life-long and faithful friend. Thanks for answering all my questions. I thank God for you!

I am thankful to the Nyree Publishing Company. Thanks especially to Kennisha Thornton for championing this whole process and for being patient with me as I asked numerous questions.

I also want to give special thanks to the very talented Cover Artist Krishna Designs and for the interior Design which was especially done by Devyn Maher, both from Nyree Press and Ingram.
To my son Simbarashe, thank you for your encouragement, and to my daughter Shekinah, thank you for being a source of inspiration. Being your mom is the best job I have had. I love you both dearly.

So very thankful for my grandchildren: Avianna, Zenai and Xavier.

Those I have named here and so many more unmentioned have all enriched my life beyond measure. May the Lord continue to pour blessings upon each and every one of you.
MY GREATEST THANKS TO GOD who is my all in all.

Pictures

My Vimbainashe before she was sick

My sister Alpha and me

My gratduation day

*My brothers Obadaih Kudzai & Jacob who died in
2003 and 2006 recpectively*

Me and Felix at an event

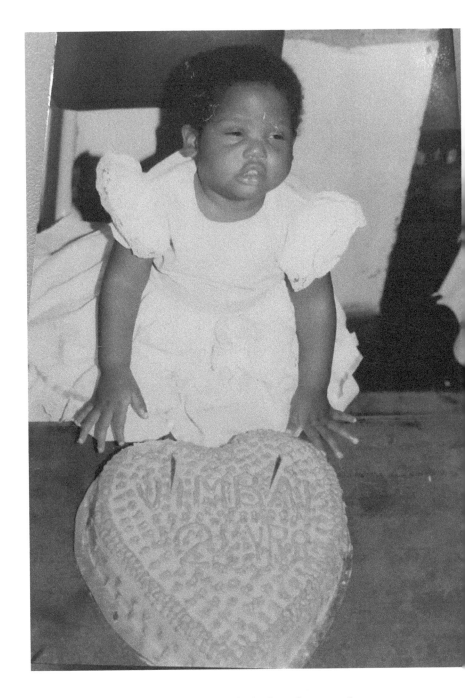

Vimbainashe four months before she passed away

Shekinah at her Father's memorial

They've got spirit

Providence Classical School dialectic students recently gathered donations from schoolmates during the school's annual Spirit and Service Week. The classes raised more than $200 to help sponsor a child in a developing country to receive a Christian education through the Association of Christian Schools International. Back row, from left: Alice Chidzero, Megan Lorincz, Taylor Henry, Sophie Quiram, Joshua Sparks, Christopher Cordasco and David Frye. Front row: Isobel Bishop, Destiny Pacella, Elizabeth Henry, Irina Richards, Caleb Monfreda and Alexander Svinicki. PHOTO COURTESY OF PROVIDENCE CLASSICAL SCHOOL

The amazing kids who isnpired me to write this book